On His Royal Badness

Published by 404 Ink Limited
www.404Ink.com
@404Ink

Editing: Heather McDaid
Typesetting: Laura Jones
Cover design: Luke Bird
Interior illustrations: Casci Ritchie
Co-founders and publishers of 404 Ink: Heather McDaid & Laura Jones

Print ISBN: 978-1-912489-32-9
Ebook ISBN: 978-1-912489-33-6

Printed and bound in Great Britain by Clays Ltd, Elcograf S.p.A.

404 Ink acknowledges support for this title from
Creative Scotland via the Crowdmatch initiative.

LOTTERY FUNDED

On His
Royal Badness

The Life and Legacy of Prince's Fashion

Casci Ritchie

Inklings

Contents

Introduction   1

Chapter 1:
Leg Warmers   9

Chapter 2:
Trench Coat   17

Chapter 3:
Cloud Suit   29

Chapter 4:
Heels   39

Chapter 5:
Polka Dots   49

Chapter 6:
Butt-Out   57

Chapter 7:
Chain Hat   69

Chapter 8:
Rave   77

Chapter 9:
Super Bowl   85

Chapter 10:
Third Eye   91

Conclusion   101

References   *107*
Acknowledgements   *116*
Further Reading   *118*
Print your own Prince   *119*
About the Author   *120*
About the Inklings series   *121*

Introduction

Prince means a million different things to millions of different people. In his 57 years on this earth, Prince achieved stratospheric success as a recording artist, selling over 150 million records worldwide and leaving behind a prolific legacy as a trailblazer of popular music. Prince's artistry remains limitless, and through performance, lyrics and fashion, he challenged conventional notions of hegemonic masculinities within popular culture. Firmly in control of his image both on and off stage, the musician's distinct wardrobe rewrote contemporary perceptions of how Black male musicians should look, sound and behave. Each look was a visual embodiment of his artistry, from ornate ear cuff down to bespoke heel. The clothing was just as integral as his music. In learning about Prince's sartorial legacy, we can learn more about Prince both as an artist and individual, and more so how his fashion interacted with and rebelled against the world around.

Prince was devoted to the art of dressing. Fearless in style experimentation, he did it all: belly tops, 4-inch heels, turtlenecks, unitards, pussy bows, silk pyjamas, DIY trench coats, kaftans, cowl necked jumpsuits, sports jerseys, corsets, zoot suits, hip chains... The man was versatile. Tactility was key within his clothing; playing with a diverse range of unconventional menswear fabrics such as PVC, lace, mesh, brocade, spandex, fringe and lamé. He championed the use of technologically advanced second-skin fabrics such as modal and digital-printed silk jerseys. Importantly, Prince's clothing had to move with the artist, whether that was 10 feet up in the air mid-split or a 3am after the after-show party. Societal limitations of twentieth-century menswear did not register on Prince's style radar. Throughout his life he was known to borrow clothing from his lovers and openly buy off-rack womenswear – it simply did not matter to him, he effortlessly made the garments look good regardless. He immersed himself in fashion magazines from all over the world, creating his tear-off scrapbooks of personal favourites to send to designers. As an artist, he understood the importance of personal style, especially as a mode of universal communication and commodity to his fans. Later in his life, Prince dropped hidden album announcements by literally wearing them, such as the NAACP Image Awards *3121* monochromatic jacket in 2005. Prince created his own unique lexicon of fashion, remaining true to himself regardless of trend or industry influence.

I feel strongly that Prince's transgressive acts of dress warrant further exploration, discussion and acknowledgement within fashion studies and beyond. Whilst critical attention has rightfully been paid to his music, background and identity, there remains comparatively little focusing specifically on Prince's style; *On His Royal Badness* will hopefully form part of this ongoing conversation. I will examine the self-created style of Prince through sequential eras, focusing on key garments worn in music videos such as the cloud suit worn in 'Raspberry Beret' and pivotal live performances, including the Super Bowl XLI halftime show. A focus will be placed on the stories behind these looks, and the wider context within which many of them sit. Each chapter will focus on a particular outfit, garment or accessory and will chronologically chart Prince's developing style, inspirations and influences on contemporary culture. This is by no means a comprehensive study of Prince's extensive wardrobe, more like a greatest hit compilation. Let's class this as The Hits Disc One for the time being.

So why am I spending all my free time researching what was inside Prince's wardrobe? Quite simply, I love Prince. He has remained a constant companion throughout my life. Some of my earliest memories oddly enough feature Prince thanks to my parents' eclectic music tastes (Cypress Hill, Skunk Anansie, George Michael, Cocteau Twins, John Lee Hooker … and Prince). I can remember squishing my face up to the television, the screen static bubbling away on my grubby little hands as I watched Prince's scandalous MTV Video Music Awards performance of 'Gett Off'. Yes, the one where his bum is out. Of course, Prince's music is key to my adulation of the artist, but I am equally enamoured, nay obsessed, with Prince's radical self-expression through personal style. Prince's overt displays of unapologetic glamour similarly resonated with me alongside my teenage discovery of Old Hollywood femme fatales. People did not look like Bacall or Prince in the real world, but perhaps it was possible? I remember the first time I watched *Purple Rain*, I think around the age of fourteen. Watching Prince writhe on stage, dripping in sweat and rhinestones, I wondered why my parents did not let me in on that particular little secret. People really could look like that?

Discovering that people dressed like that, that I could dress like that, was hugely influential to me and cemented my obsession with vintage clothes, and only strengthened my love of Prince. Charity shops became dream destinations after school where I would hunt high and low for any remnants of 'Sex Shooter' style outfits (I ended up with a pile of scratchy nylon 1980s teddies from Marks and Spencer), amassing a collection of costume jewellery, lace and 1980s polyester finery. As I progressed through high school and onto university, I chose to study fashion design, sticking up print outs of The Purple One in my studio space. I made life-long friends on the second night of staying in halls of residence thanks to my trusty Prince DVD collection. An excellent icebreaker! I went on to study fashion at postgraduate level, completing a MA in lingerie design and MLitt in dress and textile histories with Prince's influence never far away.

Shortly before Prince passed in 2016, I began to seriously dig deeper into Prince's fashion, realising that very little context and oral history had been collected. I began to interview Prince affiliates, scour auction sites for historical clothing sales and watch hours and hours of Prince footage (it's a hard life), trying to piece together the life of Prince through clothes. I have presented my purple research at various academic conferences across the UK, Europe and America; my research has also been published in books and peer-reviewed journals (more on that at the end, for those interested!). The first stepping-stones in a lifetime of collating the history of a sartorial icon.

I made my own purple pilgrimage to the Twin Cities in 2018. To this day, I still cannot believe I got that chance to visit Minneapolis, Prince's home city. Everywhere I turned there were signs of the home-town hero; cashiers with immaculate metallic purple manicures embellished with tiny Love Symbols; the Minneapolis Sound pouring out from local bars and restaurants 24/7; strolls through Uptown; an Uber driver who used to hang with musician Morris Day. His presence was felt was everywhere. As fans flocked to Paisley Park, Prince's iconic studio complex and home, I saw fathers and daughters adorned in lace, best friends dressed in matching *Lovesexy* ensembles, lone travellers meeting new friends proudly wearing customised denim jackets, meticulously hand-painted with purple iconography. Even in death, Prince's impact could be seen and felt. Through fashion, he created a visceral visual conversation that all fans could understand. Witnessing this display of reverence and adoration through clothing and self-expression was incredibly moving for me. This is where I truly realised the lasting impact that Prince's fashion has made within the lives of millions of people.

In an attempt to marry up my past life as a fashion student and everyone's desire to dress The Purple One up I have included some hand-drawn paper-dolls and coordinating outfits to tap into your creative juices along the way. I encourage you to douse these pocket-sized Prince's in glitter, colour outside the lines and string them all up next to your bed. I mean it – pictures, please. This, along with my research into Prince's sartorial universe, is my small way of giving thanks to His Royal Badness for all the sweaty nights on the dancefloor; sing-a-longs in bubble baths, failed dress-ups and constant self-discovery through his art.

Chapter 1:
Leg Warmers

Freshly signed with Warner Bros in a landmark six-figure recording deal, Prince is photographed by Robert Whitman on the streets of Minneapolis in the of Autumn 1977, the young musician captured on the cusp of unimaginable stardom. We see a young Black man dressed typically in the funkified bohemian style popular of the '70s – fashionable flares, chunky platforms, denim jacket, conservative knitwear and prominent afro. Just your typical fashion-conscious young teen. Although it was clear there was something enigmatic about the charismatic boy wonder from Minneapolis, at this stage Prince was not dressing in his now-legendary exuberant manner. Unique styling is, however, present within these photos – Prince's eclectic jewellery collection including hearts, stars, crucifix chains and pendants, a solid ID bracelet, a pinkie ring and his now-signature quirk of layering upper body garments.

Twin Cities Pioneer Press reported, 'Prince plays a number of instruments and sings, but has not been seen in performance in the Twin Cities', the explanation being that his 'ambition was to be a national recording star and he did not want to wear out his talent in local clubs.'[1] Minneapolis had to wait a while for the homegrown talent to make an appearance as a signed artist. Nearly a year after the release of his debut album *For You* in April 1978, Prince made his debut on a local stage with two benefit concerts at the Capri Theater (a former picture house in North Minneapolis still active today) on 5-6 January 1979.

Prince appeared to have rummaged through some of the city's eclectic thrift stores for the formative performances, wearing second-hand decorative button-down blouses and vests more reminiscent of the later 1960s and early 1970s style. Visually, Prince looked more or less like a typical fresh-faced musician of the time, dressed in familiar hand-me-downs from the bygone counter-culture that inspired him greatly as a child. Both nights he performed in skintight denim jeans, a rarity when we now think of Prince's expansive and often unorthodox wardrobe. Prince was known to favour bespoke clothing designed and created solely for his vision and unique frame. This was a creative practice demonstrated from an early age where, as recalled by Prince's cousin Charles 'Chazz' Smith (drummer of Prince's first band Grand Central), the young musician commissioned local schoolgirls to sew customised fashions for Grand Central.[2] Jeans were accessorised with ribbed woollen leg warmers worn high upon his thighs, paired with chunky heeled boots – more cowboy boot than the elegant pump we have grown accustomed to. The musician's stage presence was clear for all to see from the get-go. *Minneapolis Star* journalist Jon Bream attended both events, writing that Prince, 'strutted across the stage with grand Mick Jagger-like moves and gestures. He was cool, he was cocky, and he was sexy.'[3] Fashion historian Valerie Steele remarked on the period, 'The early 1970s "funkification" … simply accentuated the blatantly erotic, in-your-face sexual possibilities of dress. For example, enormous flares in the trousers legs served to focus the eye on the contrasting ultra-tight fit around the crotch and bottom'.[4] Up to this point, Prince's clothing had largely echoed popular youth styles of the times including bell-bottom flares, Santana-esque stacked platform boots and thrift store finds. What made Prince different from the offset was his unwavering sense of self and effortless style, an attribute former classmates remarked upon whilst Prince was a student of Central High School in 1972, wearing 'globular afro and wispy moustache … dress shirt with huge collar points, baggy pants, platform shoes and neckbands.'[5] Chris Moon, a record producer who helped Prince shape his musical persona, described the performer as 'painfully, painfully shy and extremely introverted'.[6] From Prince's deal signing in 1977 to 1979, there was an apparent change in both his performance style and appearance and his distinctive legwarmers played a major role in this refashioning.

Originating as preventative performance wear for dancers hoping to avoid painful cramps, leg warmers shifted from functional to fashion in the 1970s. It would appear Prince's leg warmers could have appeared from a place of functionality, a byproduct of growing up taking dance lessons and living in notoriously bitter Minnesota. Reportedly the city saw temperatures dip to as low as -33°C in January 1979[7] – no wonder he needed those woolly additions. A fashion article in *The Minneapolis Star* in January 1979 raved about the merits of layering garments (oddly, this seemed a new concept to the newspaper) during a typically cold Minnesotan winter. The writer suggested various pairings including, '…a combination of knitted leg warmers over blue jeans from ankle length to thigh and a wool knit cardigan buttoned over a cotton turtleneck sweater…'.[8] Did Prince pick up some practical wardrobe advice from the popular local paper? Perhaps the definitive choice to wear leg warmers high over his jeans, even whilst on stage, was a byproduct of a Minnesotan well-versed with plummeting temperatures? Interestingly, Prince held onto those leg warmers (or a similar pair) and loaned them to his fiancée Susannah Melvoin during one particularly cold day in 1986 who remarked on their well-loved appearance.[9]

Unfortunately, the performances themselves were far from perfect. As a result, Prince and his band received a monumental set back from the record executives who did not think they were ready to tour that summer. This massively knocked Prince's confidence and resulted in the next few months focusing on band rehearsals and finessing stage personas for all the musicians involved. Finally, after months of intense practice and preening, Prince and the band kicked off the *Prince* tour at The Roxy Theatre, West Hollywood on 26 November 1979. With the US tour in full motion, the band looked decisively different with a more eclectic juxtaposition of styles apparent on stage. Each musician was beginning to form their own individual style, something that Prince would go on to perfect with the formation of The Revolution in the coming years. Dressed in a tight striped t-shirt that accentuated his physique, Prince stripped down to monochromatic zebra print bikini briefs and matching distressed top made by Sylvia Cymone.[10] The leg warmers remained but now were worn over bare legs. In the absence of denim, the dark leg warmers now appeared to mimic female stockings minus the garter belt. Prince was no longer the 'every man', dressed slightly eccentrically in a frenzy of second-hand finds. Paired alongside his kohl-lined Bambi eyes, soft muscular body and flowing relaxed hair, Prince now teetered somewhere within the gender binary. He represented the other, something visually confrontational to traditional hegemonic masculinity, an emerging representation of Black masculinity not widely seen within performers of the era.

Progressively throughout the tour, Prince peeled away layers, experimenting with revealing fabrics such as spandex and gaudy animal print faux fur fit for the wild stage persona he was honing during these performances. Prince kicked, gyrated and prowled the US stages in this scandalous combination early on the tour before going fully topless, pouring himself into spandex and ultimately stripping down to bikini briefs and 'stockings'. Recurring tour outfits consisted of metallic spandex, delicate waist chains, satin blouses and matching posing pouches – and that was just Prince. Childhood friend and bassist André Cymone thrashed out on stage dressed in cherry red cowboy boots and clear vinyl trousers that steamed up nightly during shows. Guitarist Dez Dickerson wore skin-tight bondage trousers adorned with zips and chains. Cymone stated that along with bespoke designs, including the group's infamous trench coats, made by his seamstress sister Sylvia, the band were buying a lot of their clothing from the legendary New York alternative street wear hotspot Trash and Vaudeville that dressed the who's who of punk royalty including Debbie Harry, The Clash, Iggy Pop, and The Ramones.[11] Prince's encased thighs represented transgression, a rebellion against gendered clothing in line with the DIY punk aesthetics.

As Prince's popularity increased, his music grew steadily more confrontational, addressing social injustices, sex and utopian living. What started as a functional, fashionable accessory for the cold Minnesotan climate eventually morphed into a visual innuendo, mirroring the coy yet sexually suggestive lyrics of the musician's sophomore album *Prince* (1979). Within a few short months, Prince had fully crystallised his vision for his band and the confrontational *Dirty Mind* record was released in October 1980, with Prince sneering salaciously on the front cover in nothing but a pair of bikini briefs, used trench coat and – you guessed it – leg warmers masquerading as stockings.

Chapter 2:
Trench Coat

Close your eyes and think of Prince (keep it clean). Most of you, whether you are die-hard purple fam or a curious newbie, will conjure up the image of Prince, the star of rock-musical masterpiece *Purple Rain* (1984), all silver-studded and frilled. *Purple Rain* is the story of The Kid (played by Prince), an emerging musician from Minneapolis, who is tormented both on and off stage by troublesome relationships in his life and a thirst for stardom. The Kid is now widely regarded as Prince's most iconic look – the purple trench coat. Solidifying Prince within our pop culture consciousness, both the film and corresponding soundtrack propelled the musician to new stratospheric heights of stardom.

By the time *Purple Rain* hit the cinemas in July 1984, Prince was only just becoming a mainstream success, certainly not a performer that warranted his own feature film. Prince's self-belief made it happen.

The world was introduced to The Revolution (Wendy Melvoin (guitar/vocals), Brown Mark (bass/vocals), Lisa Coleman (keyboard, piano and vocals), Matt 'Doctor' Fink (keyboard/vocals) and Bobby Z (drums)), Prince's band that underpin the plot's tumultuous storyline. Catapulting everyone into mainstream success almost overnight, the film took a staggering $7,766,201 during the opening weekend. *Purple Rain* would go on to internationally make $68,392,977, securing the place of 12th highest grossing film of the year, millions of dollars more than *The Terminator* and *Red Dawn*.[1] Not bad for an industry newcomer.

The film perfectly plays into Prince's own self-crafted origin story, alluding to the musician's upbringing in Minneapolis but with added Hollywood glitter and grit. The city played as much a starring role in the film as Prince and The Revolution. Prince's Minneapolis lured in thousands of tourists following the film's release, all eager to experience the infectious Minneapolis Sound – a sub-genre of music which blended funk, rock, new-wave and synth – in person. First Avenue, a now-legendary music venue in downtown Minneapolis is central to the film. Prince frequented the club before filming, explaining to *Rolling Stone* in 1985, 'Before *Purple Rain* […] all the kids who came to First Avenue knew us, and it was just like a big, fun fashion show. The kids would dress for themselves and just try and look really cool. Once you got your thing right, you'd stop looking at someone else. You'd be yourself, and you'd feel comfortable.'[2]

Purple Rain was brought to life visually by the fashions and styles of the rising musicians. Before the release of the film, Prince was getting increasingly serious about his look, employing former Earth, Wind & Fire designer Louis Wells and his assistant Vaughn Terry Jelks during the *1999* era to create bespoke looks for the band.[3] Costume designer Marie France also joined the design team just a few weeks before production began and was shocked when she realised there was barely enough outfits for the band members. A dazzling array of garments are worn by Prince throughout the film including provocative stage ensembles, motorcycle gear and a teeny tiny white vest. Costumes worn in the film evoke the varying subcultural styles popular in the early 1980s and demonstrate the inherent relationship between fashion and music which was growing with the advent of MTV.

The look worn by Prince during the film's emotive performance of 'Purple Rain' of course is what remains in many people's minds. Prince wore a white ruffled blouse, tight black trousers, heels and purple trench coat that commanded as much stage presence as the guitar solo. Direct lineage can be seen between the pin-tucked dress shirt worn during the 1981 *Controversy* era and *Purple Rain*'s New Romantic blouse. France recalled the blouse was one of the first garments she designed following her initial meeting with the musician:

> 'I actually made a sketch of the ruffle shirt on the spot. One thing I had noticed in his music videos was that he was wearing one of those kinds of tacky tux shirts, and I said, "You need something much better than that. You need something you know, more Prince-like, literally." So, I thought of the romanticism of the 18th-century ruffled shirts and made some quick sketches.'[4]

The blouse featured a slightly puffed sleeve, gathered twice at the bicep and forearm and finished with an ornate frilled cuff, often worn with costume cabochon cufflinks. An expressive faux jabot is worn under an over-sized gathered stand collar, fastened tightly with pearl buttons. This style detail was fundamental to the New Romantic trend of historicism in clothing. Instead of heaving bosoms, Prince often ripped open his Casanova blouse on stage, exposing his sweaty chest to thousands of adoring fans. This proved much more positively received than his early crotch flashing days. For the subsequent tour, the shirt was reproduced in black, purple, red and white sheer lace and was accessorised with a jumble of rhinestone, pearl and metal chains. The addition of the ruffled shirt was an important inclusion in Prince's look and has continued to be replicated since its birth on screen. Before *Purple Rain*, Prince had experimented with the upper half of his wardrobe, pairing the trench coat with off the rack pin-tucked tuxedo shirts, dicky bows and bare skin, but the ruffled blouse signaled a shift in Prince's production levels. This was a bespoke garment made exclusively for the musician. What resulted was a heralding of Prince's softening sexuality, however still ambiguous, in comparison to the perverse punk provocateur of the early 1980s.

Prince's pert peach features heavily in the film thanks to the obscenely tight trousers worn both on and off stage. The trousers acted a base for much of Prince's 1980s wardrobe, with a slim high-waist, elasticated side-seam and gathered from the knee below with stirrup detailing. Nipping in Prince's minuscule waist even further, contrast buttons were strategically placed along his diagonal waist front; the buttons also fell down the side seams of the trousers in opposing size. More often than not, the trousers were black, but throughout the tour, the costume team dreamed up a myriad of florid brocades, damasks and laces to pair with matching trench coats or matador style jackets. This was a signature design staple that Prince continued to wear for much of the decade with proteges such as Sheila E and Sheena Easton also modelling (or sharing) pairs. Surviving today, these trousers are often found with reinforced crotches and repaired inner leg seams to withstand Prince's regular stage pounding and crotch-ripping dance moves. Looking back at Prince's forays into spandex and leg warmers, the ruched trousers could be seen as a natural progression from these early style experimentations.

By the time *Purple Rain* was released, the purple trench coat was in its final stages of finesse, following four years of rotation in Prince's wardrobe. Initially, the beige trench coat appeared as an off the rack army-surplus store purchase for the *Dirty Mind* era, accessorised with posing pouch, heels and those leg warmers masquerading as women's stockings again. During live performances Prince would spin, kick and gyrate with the trench coat flying open, flashing his lewd undergarments and bare flesh to the audience. Married with the album's risqué lyrics and taboo subject matters, Prince's confrontational appearance was a defiant act against hegemonic masculinities. In appearing on stage in perceived women's undergarments whilst simulating sex acts and singing lyrically ambiguous songs of explicit sexual nature, Prince was deliberately encouraging questions about his own sexual orientation. Encouraging notoriety early on his career, Prince firmly established himself as popular music's 'Other'. Unlike the intergalactic masks of '70s David Bowie, Prince did not create characters – his otherness remained strictly of this planet.

This display of lustful gluttony, impish irreverence and euphoric liberation felt dangerous yet wholly irresistible to the musician's increasingly mainstream pop audience. As Prince's look developed, the trench coats were altered in colour (dyed cornflower blue then eventually lavender purple) and festooned with fringe, chains, rhinestones and pin-badges. The release of *1999* saw Prince's trench coat reproduced in flashy purple lamé, a woven fabric with metallic fibres that came alive under lights. By this point, Prince was wearing early prototypes of the ruched button waisted trousers and was experimenting with the Eighties makeup staple – blown out fuchsia eyeshadow.

As instantly recognisable as Michael Jackson's sequined glove, David Bowie's 'Life on Mars?' ice-blue suit or Madonna's conical bra, Prince's purple trench coat is forever affiliated with the musician and encapsulates the look and sound of the 1980s. The garment is representative of the musician's personal growth following his experimental years spent in the public eye. He understood the importance of fashion, especially when it came to communicating to a wider audience and *Purple Rain* required a cohesive, unique look. Bobby Z, Prince's drummer from 1978 to 1986, recalled the introduction of the coat and its perceived role in Prince's stratospheric rise to fame:

'For me, the signal was the purple trench coat... we were coming from shopping at used clothing stores and digging through barrels, and then the symbolism of the purple trench coat was, "this is serious business". I knew he was going for it then.'[5]

For filming, Marie France altered the pre-existing trench coat fabric, investing in high-quality silk that photographed better under studio lights. The purple trench coat gets a lot of screen time in the movie – billowing behind the musician as he rode through the streets of Minneapolis on his customised Honda CM400A win-cylinder motorbike. Fetishising the garment, Prince flipped the military connotations, traditionally steeped in decades of heteronormative displays of masculinity and subverted this by wearing it alongside bare flesh and layers of feminine lace and ruffles. As a fan, you could easily replicate Prince's look by visiting your local army surplus store and customising your coat just like the many variations worn by The Revolution. In shedding his dangerous punk provocateur image, Prince was packaging himself up under a new sartorial guise, a clash of '60s culture rock god and 18th-century Lothario, dusted in rouge and glitter.

On 29 December 1984, *The Star Tribune* reported the impact Prince and *Purple Rain* had played on Minneapolis's economy. Local retailers enjoyed a rise in Prince-affiliated goods including clothing and accessories:

'Tatters Clothing sold a lot of lace gloves and purple bow ties and cummerbunds. March 4th noticed a run-on purple sunglasses and accessories, while J.J. Flash, the Arcade and Lenny's moved dozens of purple boots, shirts and pants this week and even sold some purple items to Prince's stepfather.'[6]

The film's influence was felt wider, with designers Wells and Jelks releasing Purple Wear, a clothing line inspired by the film's costumes that were sold in American youth fashion retailers such as Merry Go Round. The collection consisted of replicas of Prince's screen-worn wardrobe including his motorcycle jacket and coloured variations of the frilled blouse. There are very few examples of these garments remaining, but the original motorcycle jacket was sold by Julien's Auctions for $37,500 in 2018.[7]

Music scholar Rupert Till argues that *Purple Rain* 'helped to create the perception of a legendary Prince that no longer had to be bound by reality and could rise to iconic status'.[8] Interestingly the clothing he wore as The Kid does not feel like costume; instead, the garments are generally accepted as part of Prince's eccentric everyday wardrobe as a musician. It could be due to his obsessive work patterns that Prince was always 'on', dressing largely the same as his on stage persona. This idea of reluctant acceptance of Prince's own unconventional style deviations can be traced back to the expansive triumph of *Purple Rain*. Journalist David Denby reviewed his performance in the film, mocking the musician's unusual appearance:

> 'The tiny fop hero of Minneapolis wears black breeches, white silk shirts with ruffles, and white stock ties hanging to his belly; he has long black curly hair, a thin, libidinous mustache over wet lips, and plenty of liner around the eyes. He looks, perhaps, like one of the minor characters from an MGM period picture of the '30s – a disreputable musketeer, or a tiny, decadent minion of the court of a mad king played by Robert Morley.'[9]

Denby goes on, eventually proclaiming, 'No one this short trying this hard to be sexy should be able to get away with it. But Prince does – when he sings.'[10] Dressing as The Kid allowed Prince to challenge gender norms, racial stereotypes and sexuality in a way that was palatable for the MTV masses he was now finally performing for. His unique artistry was now part of the mainstream and through lashings of mascara, the click of 4-inch heels and silk ruffles, Prince was redefining Black masculinity, on a global scale. Whilst *Purple Rain* is largely regarded as his most celebrated works, this was Prince only just getting started at the age of 25.

So, what do you wear to follow up *Purple Rain*?

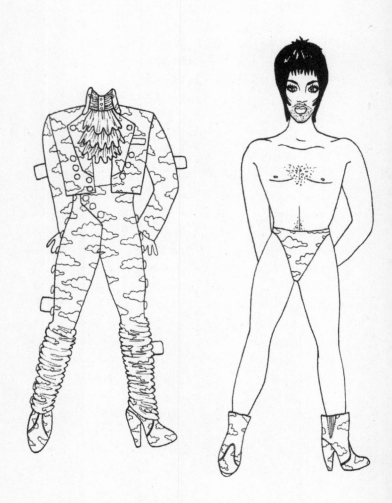

Chapter 3:
Cloud Suit

Just over two weeks after completion of the highly successful *Purple Rain* tour, Prince released his seventh studio album *Around the World in a Day* on 22 April 1985. Sonically and visually light-years away from the heady New Romantic opulence of *Purple Rain*, the follow up saw Prince experiment with world instruments and melody, resulting in a psychedelic pop trip. Lyrically, the music centred around his deep-rooted turmoil between spirituality and sex. During this period, little visual evidence of Prince's emerging style is available, with the musician releasing his eighth album, *Parade*, just under a year later. What we do see in the limited images and live performance videos is a transitional phase where Prince is combining the lurid psychedelic fabrics worn during the *Purple Rain* tour and mixing it with a baggy beige overcoat, dark shades, crop tops and Andalusian style wide-brimmed black hat. This sartorial flux signalled a shift in

Prince's creative output, establishing he was not prepared to rehash what had gone before – innovation was always on the fore front of his mind.

Aesthetically the album cover *Around the World in a Day* was a huge departure. This was no sequel to *Purple Rain*. Artist Doug Henders had worked with Prince previously to create the stylised visages featured in the bedroom of The Kid, and 'When Doves Cry' music video. Henders' former military background as a cartographer resulted in a signature camouflage layered style that worked harmoniously with the numerous individual images and symbols requested by Prince to be represented within the album cover.[1] The prismatic universe depicted on the cover art came directly from Prince's imagination; he handed Henders a 'laundry list' of sixteen drawing requests all laced within symbolic meaning.[2] A yellow ladder shoots off into the perfect blue sky and fluffy clouds, a ginger-haired child is carried off into the air holding a psychedelic font-crammed balloon, an elderly Black man sits hunched over resting on his walking stick, a grey mullet-wearing Doctor Fink stares centre front dressed in his signature scrubs. Is that a yellow-haired Prince in a cloud-covered suit? Members of The Revolution are represented within the image, with many of the stylised illustrations directly referencing lyrics from the album such as a depiction of Wendy Melvoin as Clara Bow in a nod to 'Condition of the Heart'. This was not new to Prince, with previous albums *Controversy* and *1999* both featuring referential hidden meanings within their artwork.

Initially, Prince was hesitant to produce any music videos for the album following the grueling promo for *Purple Rain*. He eventually agreed and appeared in two of the videos for the album's singles 'America' and 'Raspberry Beret'. Prince directed the latter on set in Los Angeles in early June 1985, with the final cut featuring a whimsical animated section by Drew Takahashi. 'Raspberry Beret' is a masterclass in storytelling. Prince's vibrant songwriting paints a visceral image in our minds whenever we hear the song. It tells the simple story of falling in love whilst at your mundane day job through evocative descriptions of Prince's object of desire. Significance is placed on a popular accessory at the time – a beret – which Prince likens to as the colour of vivid raspberries. The song was reportedly inspired by French silent-movie actress Renée Adorée who was photographed in one of her more widely known movies as wearing a jaunty beret.

The beret itself has many juxtaposing meanings (much like Prince and his music) within its history within popular culture. Worn famously by revolutionaries and romantics alike, the beret evokes connotations of both liberation and authority. Prince communicates with his listener, explaining the beret is just like the ones you find at second-hand stores. Naturally, you begin to envision this other-worldly beauty, beret cocked, breezing through the protagonist's humdrum life. As a fashion student, I spent many hours scouring charity shops in the Scottish Borders trying to locate the perfect raspberry beret. But there was no beret-wearing beauty in real life; Prince was writing from his imagination, resulting in an emotive fantasy that reflected in the surreal suiting he famously wore in the music video.

Walking onto the dreamlike set, Prince sweeps through a crowd of purple hippies, dressed in an azure-blue suit covered in fluffy white clouds. On the sky-blue podium, Prince appears impish and coy, vamping it up with a series of expressive cheesecake poses, all unusually off-camera. As a viewer, you feel like an outsider looking into this magical bohemian dreamscape, with Prince never once acknowledging the audience in reality. Hypnotic energy is present throughout the music video, anchored by the rhythmic swaying motions of the string players that accompany Prince's effortless wordplay. Dancing in synchronised fashion, the audience is reflective of his Paisley Park ideals. Amongst the hypnotically swaying audience, we see dancers of different races wearing ruffle shirts and buttoned trousers straight from the *Purple Rain* movie set. A young Jackie Swanson, a friend of Prince at the time, looks like she has raided The Kid's closet as she smiles and hands Prince his infamous white cloud guitar. Linda LiPuma, his art director at Warner Bros explained,

'Whatever record he put out, [the concept] would carry on through everything: the way he dressed, every single, every ad carried the theme.'[3] Much like the First Avenue crowd, the 'Raspberry Beret' spectators represented Prince's self-created purple utopia that would soon become reality with the brick and mortar of Paisley Park. This myth-building was first most notably apparent in the *Dirty Mind* track 'Uptown' – an imaginary utopia which Prince scholar Zachary Hoskins described as 'post-gender-post racial'.[4] Apparent in all of Prince's self-made worlds were ideas of racial equality, liberation and freedom of self. He did not stop once Paisley Park was built; these spaces continued to thrive physically in venues such as his Glam Slam and 3121 nightclubs but also with online fan communities such as the NPG Club. Spaces were curated directly by Prince, and fans often had the opportunity to buy branded merchandise and fashion designed by the musician. Reflected within the crowds of 'Raspberry Beret' is variations of the singer: a Prince fan would of course dress like Prince.

For the album's listening party, Wendy and Lisa helped create the desired vibe, both women appeared in silk pyjamas and scattered the dimly lit room with rose petals before Prince arrived, also dressed in his silk nightwear.[5] In this dreamscape, the artificial sky is painted an abnormally vivid blue with marshmallow fluffy clouds suspended in motion in the backdrop. Prince remains frozen in a surreal skyscape that mirrors his atmospheric attire. By mirroring the set with his cloud suit, Prince positions himself wholly in this self-created world, placing his artistic vision central to the design of his self-created universe.

The cloud suit can be viewed as an important part of Prince's sartorial legacy due to its notoriety of course, but also its unusual place within his wardrobe. The two-piece suit and matching heels are abundantly decorated with hand-painted white clouds. Visually the suit is near identical to the silhouette and design details of the lurex suit covered in intricate Paisley motifs worn in the 'When Doves Cry' music video. Uniquely, the cloud suit stands alone due to its surreal painterly print. Nature's diversity has inspired fashion for centuries with embroidered landscapes, printed night-skies and shorelines all depicted within our clothing. Perhaps the psychedelic inspirations behind the album are also reflected in the expressive print. It is unclear who designed the cloud suit, but costume designers Louis Wells, Vaughn Terry Jelks and Marie France were all still known to be working with the musician in some capacity at this time. Helen Hiatt also joined the team as wardrobe manager and costume designer during this period, but it remains likely that Chicago born, Jim Shearon expertly cut the pattern for the suit. Looking at the outfit in relation to his expansive wardrobe, the design remains wholly unique, in particular the whimsical hand-painted print that Prince seldom returned too. The DIY aesthetic of the suit is a reminder of Prince's cut and paste thrift store beginnings and indicates a shift in the quality and production of his clothing. Alongside the *Purple Rain* psychedelic tour designs, the suit can be viewed as one of the first tailored suits made for the singer. From this point on, Prince and his design team would refine his silhouette through a series of tailoring experiments, a design blueprint that remained with the musician until his passing.

I found myself standing in front of the suit in a surreal moment back in 2017 during a visit to the My Name is Prince exhibition at The O2, London. Physically seeing such an iconic outfit, devoid of its wearer was incredibly moving, particularly due to the undeniable presence felt of its owner. No one else could have worn that suit. Echoing the song's immersive narrative, Prince's outfit tells its own story, reflective of the musician's rapidly changing visual and musical style. Today the suit remains one of Prince's most celebrated outfits, with its handcrafted clouds popping up everywhere from the catwalk of Virgil Abloh's Louis Vuitton Autumn/Winter 2020 menswear collection to high-street knitwear.

Hot off the success of his previous 'era', it could have resulted easily in a re-hash of purple textiles, but Prince's decisive artistic intentions knew he had to step away and move into his next stylistic era. Whilst *Around the*

World in a Day did not have a specific look or colour palette, it allowed Prince a brief moment of style experimentation before he embarked on the next phase of his career. The cloud suit may have been utterly alien when viewed alongside his sartorial output, and yet – as with everything he wore – remains so sublimely Prince.

Chapter 4:
Heels

'Once upon a time, in France, there lived a bad boy named Christopher...' [1]

It will come as no surprise to most of you that His Royal Badness adored a high heel, smouldering on elevated custom boots for the entirety of his career. Prince's heel collection is so impressive that Paisley Park have recently opened 'The Beautiful Collection' – an exhibition showcasing over 300 pairs of the singer's shoes, and that is only a small part of his vast collection. *Under the Cherry Moon* feels like the right place to discuss his penchant for heels – the film's flamboyant glamour, lacquered spit-curls and shimmering lace are a natural companion to Prince's signature footwear. Seemingly out of place in both the modern day and the by-gone era of the film but, of course, Prince pulls it off.

Following *Around The World In A Day*, Prince went straight to work on his second feature film, *Under the Cherry*

Moon, and accompanying soundtrack *Parade* (released on 31 March 1986). Susannah Melvoin, Prince's fiancée and singer in protege band The Family, remembered Prince was incredibly excited to shoot the film, believing that the musician had been working on some of the ideas for the script since childhood.[2] After the early exit of director Mary Lambert, Prince took on the role of director to varying degrees of success. Released in July of the same year, *Under the Cherry Moon* was a flop, but amongst many fans it is celebrated as a cinematic triumph (in Prince terms).

Prince plays the part of Christopher Tracy, an international playboy who travels across the French Riviera, stealing hearts and stashing cash alongside his loyal companion Tricky (Jerome Benton). Tracy runs around the coast in custom-built heels seducing diplomat wives, daughters and mistresses until he meets debutante Mary Sharon (Kristen Scott-Thomas), and everything changes.

The film examines an interracial relationship between Tracy and Sharon that questions society's preconceived perceptions of wealth, social class and love. Prince scholar De Angela Duff describes *Under the Cherry Moon* as 'the ultimate public document of Prince as his most authentic self', highlighting that Prince's Blackness and natural wit is central to the film, allowing the audience to witness a rare insight into the star's own personality.[3] In 2016, the African American Film Critics Association recognised the significant impact left by Prince within the film-making industry:

'How many films set and actually shot in the French Riviera starred a Black man then or even star a Black man now? With 1986's *Under the Cherry Moon*, Prince inserted himself and Black men as a whole in places where society insisted, he nor his kind belong. The fact that Prince shot *Under the Cherry Moon* in black and white is no coincidence. In an actual 1930s era film, a Black man dressed like Prince's Christopher Tracy would most likely be a butler or performing usually for whites only. In many ways, he used *Under the Cherry Moon* to correct, or at least, challenge Hollywood's stereotype and that of American society at large of where Black men, in particular, belonged.'[4]

When questioned by producer Bob Cavallo about why he insisted on filming in the French Rivera, Prince replied, 'I want the people in the community to see the south of France'.[5] As highlighted by Artistic Director Melay Araya, Prince was one of the first Black owners of a film lot – Paisley Park Studios, Chanhassen, MN.[6]

In centralising his Blackness in *Under the Cherry Moon* and the subsequent opening of his own studio, Prince established himself as a pioneer in the Black film industry and would continue to champion his own community throughout his career.

If you've seen any of Prince's films, you'll be well aware he's no Cary Grant, but he knew how to captivate his audience. The relationship between Christopher and Tricky proves more tangible and believable on-screen than that of Christopher and Mary's flawed romance. This does not sour the picture at all; instead, it allows the film to explore the relationship of two Black men that may or may not be more than bosom buddies. Whilst *Purple Rain* is semi-sort-of-autobiographical, *Under The Cherry Moon* allows Prince to exercise his infamous comedic skills and bounce off his friend Benton. In fact, it is the slapstick comedy played effortlessly throughout by Christopher and Tricky that ultimately elevates the story. You can see the joy exuded by both Prince and Benton vamping it up for the cameras. A lover of classic cinema, *Under the Cherry Moon*, can be viewed as a homage to the screwball comedies of the 1930s and WW2 eras Black musicals such as *Cabin in the Sky* (1943) and *Stormy Weather* (1943). The film's costume designer Marie France even sourced original vintage fabrics for many of the film's characters from the Paramount Studio in Hollywood.[7]

Christopher Tracy's fashion parade is one hell of a wild ride, jumping from beaded flapper head-dresses to oversized black leather bomber jackets and back again. Costumes for the cast are largely inspired by jazz babies, mobsters and heartbreakers of the silver-screen yet the cultural signifiers of the 1980s such as a boom box, neon telephone and Ray-Ban sunglasses pop up unexpectedly to remind us this is a Prince film after all. We are first introduced to protagonist Christopher Tracy in the opening scenes, a vision behind a grand piano. Lit like a George Hurrell glamour portrait, Prince smoulders on screen. Hallowed high cheekbones, fluttering lashes, a pencil-thin moustache framing his full lips. In a homage to classic cinema, Tracy plays the role of the club pianist, except he looks drastically different compared to widely known Hollywood ivory tinklers, such as *Casablanca*'s tuxedo-clad Sam (played by Dooley Wilson). In fact, Tracy's look is more akin to that of the torch singer, dressed in a glittering two-piece suit, ruffled jabot, and heels. A shimmering headscarf is fastened on his forehead, the beaded scalloped edges showcasing his profile, with his curls escaping from the top. As Prince stands, we see the accessory is fastened in a knot at the nape of the head, the lengthy tassels falling dramatically down past his waist. This gesture of excessive pomp tells us all we need to know about our leading man.

Unsurprisingly, Prince's representation of a leading man is highly unconventional – a Black 'gigolo' who wears more makeup than his leading lady. A close look at the few colour production shots from the set shows Christopher Tracy's makeup in glorious detail. Prince's eyes are once again the focal point of the makeup. There is still a remnant of New Romanticism with Prince's lilac eyeshadow blended graciously outwards into fuchsia pink. His lashes are coated liberally in mascara and lined. Brows are expertly arched alongside a minutely defined moustache, nestled right above his upper lip line. His cheekbones are enhanced with a warm matte pink blush and his beauty mark finishes the look. Even when wearing a seemingly conventional black tuxedo, he subverts the narrative by wearing his hair in rigid set finger waves à la Josephine Baker. Prince's visible soft stubble, sideburns and moustache juxtapose against his exquisitely painted face. His facial hair, a traditional sign of masculinity, is expertly trimmed, brushed and gelled into place to create an unrealistic vision of glamour. Sociologist James Messerschmidt describes the male chest as a 'hegemonically masculine "sexual arena"'[8] indicating that the presence and amount of body hair can be viewed as a visual signifier of masculine identity. Distinctly on show through the film, Prince's chest hair is visibly full yet manicured, with Marie France's low-cut tailoring exposing this often throughout. Prince's personal grooming is one of the many tangible examples of his deviations of the dominant notions of masculinity.

Perhaps the decision to shoot the film in black and white hindered overall the costumes' impact on popular culture. The rare photos that exist of production show glorious lace, lustrous paisley prints, lamé and embellishment in full technicolor, and – again – that was just Prince's wardrobe. His decision to abandon the colour film with *Under The Cherry Moon* being printed and graded in black and white ultimately loses a lot of finite details, particularly in the aesthetics and styling, but the heavy makeup application does read well on screen as a homage to Old Hollywood.

Whilst Christopher Tracy's entire wardrobe warrants discussion, the unconventional suit worn by Tracy during a failed seduction with Mary is perhaps one of the most alluring on-screen outfits. The custom-made two-piece suit was designed by France and produced in a Devoré florid pattern of steel grey and black. The asymmetrical jacket featured exaggerated point sleeves; metal buttons; pocket square; a highly unusual drop extended front and cropped back and signature button adorned ruched trousers with stirrups to be worn over heels. A gold waist chain is worn with the look – a signature accessory adopted by Prince early on in his life. The alluring flash of gold decorating Prince's waist was visible throughout much of his career with early photographs showing the singer layer up various body-chains. Traditionally in Eastern societies, waist chains were indicative of femininity, spirituality, fertility, affluence and more, with both men and women wearing the style. With the counter-culture's fascination, nay appropriation, of Eastern dress, Prince's habitual wearing of the body adornment may come from the object's popularity in the later 1960s and 1970s. The definitive cut of the jacket is distinctively languid in comparison to Prince's previous tailored outfits. Around this same time, Prince's band The Family (St. Paul Peterson (vocals/keyboard), Susannah Melvoin (vocals), Jellybean Johnson (drums), Eric Leeds (saxophone) and Jerome Benton (percussion)) wore tactile pyjamas in sumptuous silks and satins. This newly formed sartorial vision harmoniously aligned with *Parade*'s minimalistic funk and wondering instrumentals.

One review from *The Village Voice* proclaimed, 'the flaming creature who calls himself Prince may be the wittiest heterosexual clown since Mae West.'[9] Comparisons between the two performers are evident, particularly in *Under the Cherry Moon*. In a similar fashion to His Royal Badness, Mae West was renowned for her voluptuous augmented figure. Using props such as corsetry, powdered wigs, and bespoke 'double-decker' heels, West engineered her extreme hourglass ideals. To increase her height (West was rumoured to be between 5 and 5'2"), she worked with footwear designers to engineer bespoke stacked high heels that would measure around 9½ inches. Both artists were not afraid of controversy, using their self-crafted mystique and indiscretions to further fuel their star power. Similarly, West was fully invested in her artistry, insisting on writing her own material and creating her stage persona 'sequin by sequin'.[10] Just like West, Prince was never found without his heels, a personal footwear choice he had favoured since a teenager when he and his cousin Chazz Smith would go hunting in Minneapolis's thrift stores for platforms just like Santana.[11] Early on, Prince wore store-bought heeled boots from brands such as Zodiac and Franco Pachetti (musical hero Miles Davis was also photographed as wearing these in *GQ* in 1970).[12] As Prince's career progressed, he began to wear short custom heel boots, firstly produced by The City Cobbler who strengthened the shoes with steel reinforcement at the bottom of the heel to stop Prince from breaking the heels during his energetic dancing. The majority of his shoes were designed by Los Angeles footwear designer Andre No. 1. Each pair cost 'upwards of a couple of thousand dollars' and, at one point, Prince was ordering between 30 and 40 bespoke heels a month from the designer.[13]

Throughout *Under the Cherry Moon*, Prince's penchant for heels is strikingly apparent, particularly set within the quasi-historical backdrop of his French Rivera. Every occasion warranted a coordinating outfit and heel; he wore heels exclusively throughout his daily life and during intensive live performances on stage where he famously leapt from high-range speakers into flawless splits.[14] Reportedly, Prince suffered chronic pain after decades of consistent heel wearing. Shortly after his passing, Vanessa Friedman suggested in *The New York Times* that Prince 'transformed the idea of men in heels to possibility from joke', suggesting that Prince's high-heeled penchant could also be equated to the sexual connotations often linked with women wearing heels.[15] Speaking to *Rolling Stone* in 1985, Prince explained his adoration of wearing heels: 'People say I'm always wearing heels cuz I'm short... I wear heels because the women like 'em.'[16]

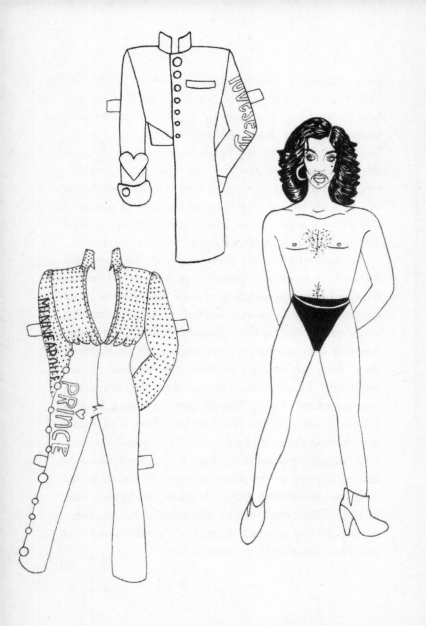

Chapter 5:
Polka Dots

Prince promises us that we will want him from his head to his feet in 'Alphabet Street', the first single from his tenth studio album *Lovesexy*, released in May 1988. And we do, thanks to his fresh spearmint polka dot ensemble. The video opens with a close-up of Prince lying on the floor, air humping along to what sounds like a Paisley Park playground rhyme. Prince wears a seafoam green blouse, unbuttoned down to his waist, decorated with contrasting black polka dots. The collar is worn flush to his neck, a signature styling detail the musician favoured for many decades to come. A low-hanging gold chain drapes around his bare neck. His inky black trousers are worn obscenely high and are rigorously tailored at the waist, creating a flat crotch closure and flowing into a soft peg-leg cut. Cartoon-sized buttons of varying width chase down both legs, matching seafoam green, of course. Prince wears his name upon his right thigh in vinyl transfer. Matching green heels, clear glitter encased Lucite cane and graphic mirrored love heart bracelet complete the look.

Later in the video, he throws on a blousy turquoise studded leather jacket (similar to the 'Kiss' jacket) to play his incredibly Eighties Model C guitar. Prince cannot resist bearing some skin and hulks out, ripping off an alphabet print shirt to reveal a hairy chest and crucifix. A white Thunderbird car is featured throughout the video, with Prince driving the vehicle dressed in a green and black jacket, personalised with the word 'Minneapolis' down the sleeve, a key garment worn throughout the *Lovesexy* '88 tour. This design detail was adopted last-minute on the first night of the tour where Prince requested Helen Hiatt to include the alterations to his jacket just an hour before the show's opening.[1]

Born the same year of *Lovesexy*'s release, indirectly I was bopping along to Prince's 'Alphabet Street' as a young girl daily, listening to the song feature as a recurring radio jingle in my Dad's Ford Mondeo (unfortunately not a Ford Thunderbird). I was unaware that the song was Prince until a chance charity shop discovery – the *Lovesexy* album cassette tape, a bargain at 50p. I remember thinking what an odd album cover. Not just the erotic cherub cover art but the distinctly Prince symbolic iconography on the tracklisting: powder blue and bubblegum pink song titles finished with graphic eyes and clashing cursive and barbed fonts.

Fashion photographer and music video director Jean-Baptise Mondino shot the album's front cover as well as the 'I Wish U Heaven' video. No comment can be passed on the *Lovesexy* album cover outfit as Prince had decided to forego his Paisley Park tailoring and go au naturel, his naked silhouette retouched digitally by Mondino and nestled amongst a blanket of orchids. Stamen fully erect. Mondino later described the final image as 'a religious image par excellence'.[2] I have to agree. *Lovesexy* marked a spiritual rebirth following the shelved release of notorious *The Black Album*, a musical project that began as a dance project for his girlfriend at the time but contained some of Prince's most sexually aggressive and dark lyrics. At the last-minute Prince pulled the project and gave the world *Lovesexy* instead. Immediately there is a prominent duality both seen and heard within the album, the musician's infinite battle between the sacred and profane, resulting in the clothed and unclothed body depicted within the artwork.

Mirroring the music, *Lovesexy* fashion was a blend of styles: sportswear, 18th-century romanticism and outlandish zoot suits straight out of Tune Town. Following on from the canary yellow zoot suit worn during the 1986 *Parade* tour, Prince further developed this subcultural style staple with the addition of signature buttons and (if possible) an uber exaggerated shoulder line. *Lovesexy* '88 was the first job for the newly formed Paisley Park wardrobe department. The tour also saw Prince's newly formed band: Miko Weaver (guitar/vocals), Levi Seacer Jr. (bass/vocals), Doctor Fink (keyboards/vocals), Sheila E. (drums, percussion/vocals), Boni Boyer (keyboard/organ/vocals), Cat Glover (dance/vocals), Eric Leeds (saxophone) and Atlanta Bliss (trumpet) dressed cohesively in complimentary uniform, in a similar vein to The Revolution prior.

BBC's *Behind the Beat* filmed a tour of Paisley Park, with a section dedicated to the complex's recently opened wardrobe department. The room is crammed with clothing rails, pattern cutters, industrial sewing machines and fabric samples pinned to the walls. Head of Paisley Park Wardrobe at the time, Helen Hiatt, is interviewed in the feature and shows off rails of the upcoming *Lovesexy* '88 tour wardrobe whilst discussing the collaborative relationship between Prince and designer. The injection of creative energy through the opening of Prince's new complex resulted in the clothing's celebratory feel, a playfulness and tactile joy that reflected *Lovesexy*'s rapturous gospel funk.

Along with the introduction of princely polka dots, one of the tour's most opulent looks was the Mozart outfit, a monochromatic ensemble consisting of a black frock coat and high-waisted trousers all produced in appliqued floral detailing. A restrained variant of the *Purple Rain* outfit, less ostentatious in colour palette and featuring a cropped structured jabot blouse, more form-fitting and graphic. A secondary historical-inspired costume featured a sportswear jersey playsuit, worn over a crisp white shirt with the word 'sound' running down the puff sleeves. A polka dot scarf was tied in a bow around his neck. Prince wore his curled hair tied back with ribbon and accessorised with white tights, Dick Whittington-style suede thigh high heeled boots and oversized acrylic cut chain belts featuring familiar iconography: hearts, peace signs, crosses completed the oddball outfit. The wardrobe acted as a hybrid of the earlier flamboyance of Prince and The Revolution but was propelled forward with the parred back colour palette, stretch fabric and developing Paisley Park silhouette.

A Vanity Fair journalist reported from behind the scenes of the *Lovesexy* '88 tour in London and described Prince's arrival look to the afterparty 'wearing lace, polka dots, an eighteenth-century ponytail' describing the musician as 'draped' in the darkness, 'a rococo mario-nette with its strings cut'.[3] In these Mozart homages, Prince appeared as a caricature of himself, the musical prodigy and Love God of the early 1980s now maturing and likening his creative work to the great composer. By aligning himself with Mozart through sartorial pastiche, Prince was knowingly building upon his past childhood mysteries of scandal, contested parenthood and child prodigy genius. His upbringing was very much present within this project, visually in the tailored shout outs to his beloved home city of Minneapolis.

When it comes to fashion, *Lovesexy* holds a special place within the purple fandom. Similar to the 'cloud suit', the *Lovesexy* wardrobe holds a distinct place within the sartorial legacy due to Prince's unexpected impish take on aristocratic dress, in that Prince looked like he was having a great time playing dress-up during this period. His clothing reflected the joyous, spirited music he created at the time with a focus on clean, graphic patterns and an ever-defining silhouette. As a result, fans recreate the pop-art polka dots and slogan details of *Lovesexy* almost as often as the *Purple Rain* ruffles and lace, something I witnessed and took part in during my Minneapolis trip.

Perhaps as Prince's early seduction suggests, the allure of the *Lovesexy* uniform is the emergence of a refinement within his wardrobe. In wearing conventionally perceived masculine garments such as button-down shirts and zoot-suits in this era Prince moves further away from the illustrious costume seen throughout the mid-1980s and begins to define his own brand of unconventional tailoring that would reach its height in the early 1990s – a New Power masculinity.

Chapter 6:
Butt-Out

Prince invited *Vogue US* for an interview and accompanying photo shoot with acclaimed fashion photographer Herb Ritts for the magazine's January 1992 edition. This was amidst the release of his thirteenth studio album, *Diamonds and Pearls*, which signalled a return to mainstream success for the prolific artist. The feature is a rare glimpse into Prince's creative world, sharing the day-to-day musician's now established Paisley Park wardrobe department and the selection process of bespoke garments from designers Giorgio Armani, Chanel, Jean Paul Gaultier and his own creations. Journalist George Kalogerakis and André Leon Talley, then creative director of *Vogue*, witnessed Prince getting ready for the shoot, reflecting in the article, 'He is a pop dandy. He has thought of everything: the stirrups, the padded lace in fine European fabrics, the custom English shoes that make his feet look like neat little hooves.'[1] The 'pop dandy' Prince era, helmed by the talents of costume designer Stacia Lang, is often revered as a glittering jewel in this sartorial legacy. Around this time Prince was sporting a look he coined 'Gangsta Glam', a fashion style expressed through the lyrics of the self-titled song 'Godfather III meets Barbarella'. This unusual marriage of film references resulted in a wardrobe of broad chalk stripes, fedoras, tailored jumpsuits and killer cat eyeliner.

The expansive 'Gett Off' Maxi Single and accompanying video cassette was released in June 1991 and consisted of six variations of the sleazy funk dance track including 'Gett Off (Houstyle)', 'Violet the Organ Grinder', 'Gangster Glam', 'Clockin' the Jizz (Instrumental)' and finally 'Gett Off (Flutestramental)'. Having your own studio stage came in handy with Prince releasing several music videos for the many incarnations of the hit song. Self-indulgent? Prince? Never. Listening and watching the various interpretations of the hit single is a compact case study on Prince's undeniable prowess, but also his ability to create a compelling aesthetic for his artistry.

His Royal Badness desecrated the MTV Video Music Awards stage on 5 September that year with the infamous performance of 'Gett Off' that now lives on in pop music infamy. Prince and the New Power Generation (Levi Seacer Jr. (guitar), Sonny T (bass), Rosie Gaines (keyboard/vocals), Tommy Barbarella (keyboard), Tony

M (rap/dancer), Kirk Johnson (percussion/dancer) and Damon Dickson (percussion/dancer) strolled onset and orchestrated a live orgy of bodies, bathed in seedy blue light, simulating multi-partnered lovemaking with Prince as the central muse. Prince performed a giant burlesque on stage without removing a single layer: gyrating, flexing and grinding in a two-piece crafted by Stacia Lang with an illusion net peephole that framed the musician's pert derrière. This was a distinct design detail that the musician requested along with the colour and fabrics requirements of yellow and lace.[2] With every thrust, the fabric stretched across his haunches, threatening to flash more skin. The citron yellow Guipure lace buttocks-bearing ensemble is now part of the global pop vernacular and heralds Prince as the eternal sexual deviant of popular music.

Mirroring the VMA's debauchery, the 'Gett Off' music video, directed by Randee St Nicholas, depicts yet another Paisley Park orgy. Newly recruited dancers Diamond (Lori Elle) and Pearl (Robia LaMorte) performed a choreographed ménage à trois with Prince in diaphanous baby dolls and femme-bot ponytails (here's where the nod to Jane Fonda's *Barbarella* come in). Style-wise it is a relatively sober affair with Prince modestly dressed head to toe in black. A hedonistic beatnik thrusting his phallic yellow Cloud guitar instrument. Wearing a scooped black velvet top, paired with black cinched trousers, his bare neck is unusually exposed. His hair is piled up in a nod to the 1950s rock and roll queer trailblazers Little Richard and Esquerita. There is something highly erotic about seeing Prince's neck and clavicles, usually hidden under crisp upturned collars. An atypical erogenous zone uncovered, something Prince displayed frequently through the (un)dressing of his chest, hips and midriff. Historically, men's clothing typically rendered the wearer tightly 'buttoned up', often removing a garment to reveal another layered garment.[3] This is distinctly different in Prince's wardrobe with the musician's preference for second skin stretch garments, the moldable textiles extending over his body in motion with ease. Slices of flesh are present in many of Prince's outfits, with the audience under no illusion undergarments exist beneath the unyielding material. In reality, they were often so taut that no undergarments could be possible for the wearer, resulting in the contours of Prince's naked body exposed, particularly around the pelvis and buttocks. Anne Hollander discussed the Neoclassical dandy in *Sex and Suit: The Evolution of Modern Dress*, explaining that the dandy favoured restraint in clothing: 'careful fit without adornments, on the other hand, emphasises the unique grace of the individual body'.[4] The uncharacter-istically chaste outfit is an example of Prince's sartorial refinement during this era. We had grown accustomed to seeing The Purple One in revealing garb, yet this fuller coverage two-piece still channeled the musician's visceral embodiment of sensuality. Simply put, he oozed sex even when trying to serve us a demure beatnik look.

Alongside his modish outfit Prince wore his hair in a durag, a head wrap originally worn by enslaved African Americans in the 19th century and later was adopted in everyday Black haircare to maintain hairstyles.[5] In the deliberate wearing of this accessory, it can be viewed as a conscious celebration and centering of Prince's Blackness along with the song's sample of James Brown's 'Mother Popcorn'. His durag was fastened tight, coaxing his curls higher and embellished with a solid gold metal variation of the Love Symbol pin, the unpronounceable moniker he used within his branding at the time.

You could easily mistake the music video for 'Gangster Glam' to be a novel infomercial for in-line skater enthusiasts but, in reality, it is another incarnation from the 'Gett Off' maxi-single, directed most likely by Prince. The video was shot at Paisley Park and the musician's Galpin Blvd house in Chanhassen and depicts Prince and the New Power Generation relaxing at home: sunbathing, doing their taxes and roller-skating. The video is very much centred around extravagant expressions heteronormative masculinity including depictions of wealth and status (fleets of sports cars, poolside living and a bevvy of women at the NPG's beck and call). Think of it as an early incarnation of *Cribs* but with more eyeliner. Within

40 seconds of the video, we see Prince in five equally astounding coordinating ensembles including poolside glam, skate wear and a slippery outfit designed for sliding down your sports car collection. Prince takes a back seat for the duration of the song, with Tony M taking the mic and literally spelling out what 'Gangsta Glam' is as Prince and the band are shown embracing this new style craze. Possibly one of his most peculiar ensembles to date is his black bikini bottoms and thick black braces look. His scant flesh is exposed even more so as the braces hoist up the briefs higher on his upper thighs. This look echoes an early fashion statement from the front cover of *Right On!* Magazine in 1979, in broad white braces, this time hoisting up red gymnastic shorts, all meticulously juxtaposed with a perfect blow-out and balmy lip. Every look remains distinct and fully realised whilst feeling part of a cohesive thematic style. Durags once again feature with three correlated examples worn styled alongside fedoras and perfectly coiffed poodle dos. Prince hams it up on set, playing up to some of the conventional gangster stereotypes but ultimately inverts the character to become wholly unique, with the addition of cosmetics, heels and a high-octane glamour. In effect this amplifies the character's performed masculinity with his own pop dandy elegance juxtaposed. Unlike his on-screen counterparts, Prince unsettles the conventional image of masculinity with an immaculately painted face, exuberant hairstyle

and towering heels. Prince personifies the modern dandy with traditional suiting materials such as graphic pinstripes and coordinating design details with Lang stating in 1991, 'he always has eight buttons on his cuffs and his trousers.'[6] This finite consideration is evidence of Prince's exemplary signature attention to detail that was particularly evident during the *Diamonds and Pearls* era with outfits accompanied with corresponding cufflinks, canes, durags and chains. His white blouse, worn open revealing his groomed chest, is tied in a perfect bow high at the waist, accentuating his tiny frame. His unique Paisley Park tailoring is evident within his pinstriped suit completed with a heavily shoulder-padded silhouette, contrasting white buttons and figure enhancing slim cut.

In stark contrast the overt machismo and heteronormative relationships displayed in 'Gangster Glam', the music video for 'Violet the Organ Grinder' (also directed by St. Nicholas) tells a different story, offering unconventional expressions of sexuality in which Prince is centred as the focal objet d'art, inviting the viewer into an inner sexual sanctum. Caged behind bars, a petite figure poses centre stage, enveloped by two golden-hued cage dancers that appear straight out of one of Prince's favourite films at the time, *Caligula* (1979). As the mystery figure opens their ornately gilded arms, they introduce themselves as 'Violet the Organ Grinder', a chain-clad masked figure with the intention of tending your sexual pleasure 24/7.

The figure's face is completely disguised under a waterfall of chunky metal chains attached to a black cap which was branded with a metal Love Symbol. This immediately gives away the identity of the elusive entity (spoiler alert – it's Prince).

An intricate mesh of gold circles and latticed chains adorn Prince's chest, the metal findings glistening against his flesh. A pair of dangerously tight cinched trousers are worn to complete the devious vision. Revisiting a similar mise-en-scène featured in the *1999* album shoot, Prince is found reclining, seemingly nude, amongst a tangle of fuchsia bed sheets. His modesty is preserved throughout the video as he lies bed bound, lustfully moaning and posing with some lovely looking grapes like a coiffured Dionysus. His skin glows amongst the warmth of berry linens, his complexion expertly painted for the Grecian Gods with a smokey doe eye rivalled only by Barbarella's Bambi stare. Prince reclaims purple with the second look of the film – a formal tailored suit and flouncy blouson, mimicking the 'Gangsta Glam' styling. The eye-popping colour contrast of juiced purple grapes and luminous Chiquita banana yellow is mouth-watering, making the song's visuals all the more lustful. Silhouetted against his erotic factory backdrop, Prince's figure cuts a defined shadow of angular shoulders, snatched waist and lean legs. Although Prince's suit does hark back to traditional menswear of the late 1940s, the silhouette is more akin to the 'mannish suit' designs worn by female actors such as Marlene Dietrich and Katherine Hepburn in the 1930s.[7] Whilst Violet sings about masturbating with their lover's stockings and brassieres, the song remains elusive to the sexual orientation of the character. More so, it is implied that the sexual orientation is not important. The character of Violet was created to provide sexual gratification, regardless of time, space or gender. Although Prince never identified as queer, his transgressive attitudes to sexuality and masculinity have impacted the queer community and formed a basis for many people's sexual awakenings.[8]

Prince's visual presentation in the music video depicts a long-standing fascination with fetish wear, with previous performances during the *1999*, *Purple Rain* and *Lovesexy* tours including chains, restraints, masks, and so on. These acts were typically fronted by the female performers in Prince's band including Jill Jones, Lisa Coleman, Wendy Melvoin and Cat Glover, with Prince adopting the role of submissive male. Violet positions Prince as both the dominant and submissive with an incessant need to 'grind all the live long day'.

By the mid-1990s, Prince's mainstream success was lessening, and it could be argued that his music, increasingly influenced by rap and hip hop, displayed varying degrees of misogyny, particularly with machismo dominance. Against the growing popularity of hip hop and the genre's aggressively heteronormative masculinities, the *Diamonds and Pearls* wardrobe was a turning point in the musician's appearance. He was prepared to change it up musically, but remained true to his own brand of erotic heteronormative dress that disrupted traditional notions of menswear. Whilst Prince's 'otherness' was perhaps not as obviously amplified as the fuchsia blusher Casanova of the 1980s, *Diamonds and Pearls* solidified Prince as an ever-expanding unconventional fashion icon for the new decade.

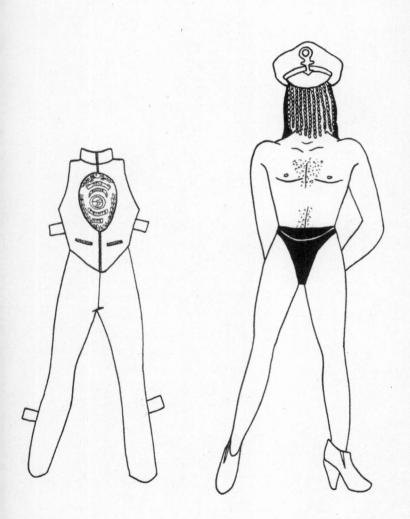

Chapter 7:
Chain Hat

Throughout his career, Prince wore many hats: bowlers, fedoras, panamas, homburgs, beanies, top hats – to name a few; but no chapeau remains as notorious as the chain hat. First popping up in the 'Violet the Organ Grinder' music video, mentioned previously, the chain hat was an indicator of Prince's life-long interest in BDSM imagery. Widely attributed to the 'My Name Is Prince' music video, the hat heralded a yet-seen combative energy within Prince's performances during the *Love Symbol* album. Released in October 1992, just over a year after the commercial success of *Diamonds and Pearls*, the genre-diverse album saw Prince feature yet more contemporary hip hop and rap along with experiments at reggae and rock opera.

Whilst still commanding the same elusive prowess as Violet in the previous year's outing, the chain hat took on a whole new meaning within the 'My Name is Prince' music video. It no longer felt sexually suggestive nor submissive, instead, when worn alongside the gritty streets of Minneapolis, the hat felt revolutionary. Filming took place in downtown Minneapolis and Paisley Park Studios and features a flustered Kirstie Alley as reporter Vanessa Bartholomew, and Lauren Green as studio anchor. Bartholomew reports 'live' during a city-wide riot following a staged Prince and the New Power Generation doppel-gänger concert. Yes, it is quite confusing. It is important to note that the video was filmed in August, just a few short months after the LA Riots, which occurred following the unjust acquittal of Los Angeles Police Department officers who used excessive force during the arrest of Rodney King, a young Black man. The brutal assault was caught on videotape and subsequently broadcast across America and the world, becoming one of the first examples of police brutality to go viral.

Worn alongside his chain hat, Prince dressed head to toe in black with gold accents, including branded Love Symbol black leather gloves and fitted funnel vest decorated with thick gold zips and what appears to be an embroidered bespoke gold New Power Generation branded Minneapolis Police Department badge. This badge was additionally used in promotional t-shirts in 1992.[1] In recreating the Minnesotan police badge, Prince was once again commenting on the ongoing social injus-tices felt at that time, King's assault particularly close to him as a Black man. Echoing the utopian rallies of 'Uptown' (1980) and 'New Power Generation' (1990), Prince made a decisive statement in disguising himself and projecting a new image of the law. The world was no longer a safe place; the people, the New Power Generation, had to take over to ensure unity for all. The top could also be seen as a stylised bullet-proof vest with its close-fitting cut and visible zips (a key feature in many Stacia Lang designs of this era).

Clutching a bespoke gold gun microphone, Prince arms himself with his music and performs on the streets of Minneapolis with the New Power Generation as the city riots. This look was strikingly more aggressive and macho in presentation than his prior expressions of masculinity. Quickly becoming one of Prince's most notable accessories, the gun microphone featured in a number of tours later in his career. When questioned about his stances on gun safety and the reasoning why he chose to perform with the gun microphone, Prince replied, 'My words of peace go in2 the gun and nullify its power'.[2]

In 2015, Prince performed a free concert Rally 4 Peace at Baltimore following the death of Freddie Gray, a 25-year-old Black man who died after sustaining several spinal injuries whilst in police custody. During the show Prince declared, 'The system is broken [...] It's going to take young people to fix it. We need new ideas, new life.

Most of all, we need new piece. And the kind of piece I'm talking about is spelled 'P-I-E-C-E.' Next time I come to Baltimore, I want to stay in a hotel owned by one of you. I want to play in a building owned and operated by one of you – I'm talking to the young people now.'[3]

The chain hat was all Prince's idea, with the musician requesting his wardrobe team to affix gold tone chains to his pre-existing policeman cap (perhaps this was the same hat worn during the *Sign of the Times* tour with the insignia removed). Lightweight aluminium chains allowed ease of movement during energetic dance moves without any discomfort to Prince.[4] On closer inspection of one example of the chain hat worn during the *Act I* tour in 1993, it would appear the hat is a modified bell crown fire department cap with a gold Love Symbol mounted to the centre. Performing with the chain hat became an integral part of Prince's live performances during the *Act I* USA and Canada (8 March – 17 April 1993) and *Act II* European tours (26 July – 7 September 1993). Opening the show, a chain clad figure masquerading as Prince would enter the stage and perform 'My Name is Prince', by the end of the song it is revealed that the masked singer was actually Mayte Garcia, New Power Generation dancer at this time. This was not the first time Prince had orchestrated switcheroos with women within his band, most notably the 'Sign of the Times' single cover art which depicts Cat Glover posing behind a large scaled mirrored heart. Many fans initially thought this was Prince; however the back cover revealed otherwise, Glover with Prince-esque hair and peach-tinted glasses, holding his guitar.

Interestingly, Stacia Lang recalled Prince requesting chain mail for his stage clothes during the *Love Symbol* album, in particular a look for the song '7'. This material was vetoed by Lang, she explained, 'If you knew Prince, he didn't not want anything rubbing too hard on his shoulders or being uncomfortable. He loved luxury, he loved being cocooned in luxury, so I said, okay, we gotta forget about the chainmail situation – I want to design something based on lace that looks sort of like chainmail.'[5] Whilst outwardly Prince appears more traditionally masculine in his clothing with the inclusion of an unexpected conservative black uniform, he subverts the machismo, as an aggressive figure dressed in heels. By this point, Prince's signature button trousers had increased in length with the heavily darted waistband now fastened high on his body, resting just under his nipples. This acted as an integrated corset within his trousers, emphasising his cinched waist and exaggerated buttocks. His signature buttons had now shrunk, with dainty contrast buttons affixed to the side seam, from calf to mid-thigh. Jackets were also cut higher, with many styles reminiscent of shrunken matador jackets in a hue of striped contrast colours. Fashion journalist Prudence Glynn wrote in great detail about the linked eroticism of the matador and American football players male silhouette, likening it to an inverted phallus. She explained, 'The matador, who has been around longer, is equally padded to enhance his manly form [...] but because his game is one of real life and death he lards himself with sequins and as much glamour as the gladiator's armour'.[6] Much like the matador, Prince's body was padded with ever expanding shoulder pads and shaped with curved darts and corseted waists. Outwardly, Prince's clothing appeared increasingly ostentatious and high femme but was this sartorial tactic to prepare him for his own battle on the stage? Overall, Prince visually became leaner and increasingly experimental with a greater defined and sculpted silhouette that looked more akin to the exaggerated curves and cursive collars of Thierry Mugler's womenswear. With the addition of heavier use of cosmetics including that whip sharp cat-eye liner, Prince's appearance was strikingly different from his contemporaries. Pressure from his record company to continue to produce mainstream pop records could have convinced Prince to dial back his exuberant personal style but he only seemed to turn the volume up.

In 1992, there were reports of Prince signing an extension deal with Warner Bros. potentially worth an astonishing $100 million; the company were keen for Prince to take a step back from quick-succession releases.[7] Growing further frustrated by Warner Bros.' inability to keep up with his prolific output, Prince became progressively disenchanted by the record company's control of his music and brand, and took action. Originally posted on Prince's website thedawn.com in February 1996, Prince reflected on his name change:

'The first step I have taken towards the ultimate goal of emancipation from the chains that bind me to Warner Bros. was to change my name from Prince to O(+>. Prince is the name that my Mother gave me at birth. Warner Bros. took the name, trademarked it, and used it as the main marketing tool to promote all of the music that I wrote.'[8]

Prince scholar Twila L. Perry discussed Prince's dispute with Warner Bros., expressing that the disagreement highlighted the 'historical and contemporary exploitation of Black musicians' with Prince likening recording contracts to slavery. When Prince later wrote 'SLAVE' across his face in 1995, in a defiant act against his record company, Perry asserts, 'he used his own Black body to send a message that linked his struggle to that of past and present African Americans'.[9] Not just an outrageous stage prop, the chain hat reasserted Prince's place within the music industry as a creative maverick. Abound in chains, the hat became a literal representation of the constraints Prince felt as a Black musician at the time, and asserted his control over his art.

Chapter 8:
Rave

At twelve years old, I spent Millennium Eve hiding behind the living room curtains in fear of the imminent threat of planes falling out the sky and crazed electric appliances taking over the world thanks to the supposed Millennium Bug. Prince, on the other hand, welcomed 2000 a few days prior to the big day with a staged concert and abundance of gold glitter hairspray.

By 1999, Prince was now known as 'The Artist' and was preparing to release his twenty-third studio album, *Rave Un2 The Joy Fantastic*. The album would be the last release to use the Love Symbol glyph before he returned to using his name on 16 May 2020 and featured appearances from Gwen Stefani, Eve, Chuck D, Ani DiFranco, and Sheryl Crow. Steve Parke, former Paisley Park photographer, captured some of Prince's more experimental fashion looks of the later 1990s. The Artist's wardrobe at this time was an eclectic mix of baseball shirts, glossy tiger print trousers, yak fur boots and ornately embroidered floor-length kaftans. Hairstyles became more diverse with Prince mimicking the multi-ponytail look worn by his cousin when she was young as well as decorated multiple plaits and bouncy feathered blow-dries.[1]

You may be wondering what Prince wore to bring in the new Millennium? Glad you asked. An electric blue metallic two-piece, with matching heels, singular gold hoop, celestial ear cuff and Y2K-appropriate glitter hairspray, of course. Created by Los Angeles designer Jose Arellanes, the two-piece comprising of a funnel neck tunic style top and high-waist bell-bottom trousers became somewhat part of Prince's everyday dress latterly in the decade. Arellanes had a store, Exit 1 on Melrose Avenue in Los Angeles, which became well known for on-screen clothing for film, television and music videos. Prince's half-brother Duane Nelson and assistant Yvette visited often, selecting designs for Prince to wear, and requesting bespoke pieces from the designer. This creative partnership would last from November 1997 to the early 2000s. Arellanes discussed Prince's relationship towards stage wear, noting that 'he was well aware of the impression he would have on stage' and felt commonly requested design details such as shoulder pads, bell-bottom trousers and turtlenecks would 'give a person a large form to their figure'. The designer thought this was perhaps why Prince favoured these styles. For each design, Arellanes was required to keep behind the fabric used and pass this onto his shoemaker Andre No. 1 to construct a head-to-toe look.[2]

Arellanes' signature style consisted of easy to wear, bold fabrics that performers loved to wear on stage. 'All the clothing I designed had the stretchy fabric which was ideal for Prince's energetic performance style. The specific stretchy fabrics I used were really comfortable and I think that's also why he liked my designs, because he felt comfortable enough to jump and dance on stage, while looking aesthetically good at the same time.' For the *Rave* outfit, Arellanes sourced an Italian bathing suit fabric with four-way stretch, this would allow for full command of his body on stage whilst still visually evoking a strong stage presence. He explained, 'Whenever I would use the fabric I used for Prince, I wouldn't use it for any other celebrity or artist's designs because of respect for him – that was the look and fabric I chose specifically for him.' Whilst designing outfits for the musician, Arellanes was always mindful on how the garments would perform on stage, 'keeping in mind the stage lighting and angles'.[3]

The outfit was worn several times by Prince in 1999, featuring prominently on the cover of the album *Rave Un2 The Joy Fantastic* and during his New Year's pay-per-view concert *Rave Un2 The Year 2000*, filmed on 18 December 1999 at Paisley Park. Packed full of influential musicians within his life such as George Clinton, Maceo Parker, Larry Graham, Rosie Gaines and Lenny Kravitz, the concert was a celebration of Prince's back catalogue and musical inspirations. The Artist confirmed to CBS' The Early Show that the concert would be the last performance of his iconic 1999 as 'there won't be no need to play it in the '00s'. That promise did not last long.

Now enjoying a fashion revival, the Y2K aesthetic mirrored the recent advancements of technology including CDs and the World Wide Web. Whilst Y2K looked to the future, popular culture exhibited high levels of anxiety about what was coming next with the threat of the Millennium Bug (see, it wasn't just me!). Fashion revisited sci-fi classics such as *Tron* (1982) as well as the year's blockbuster *The Matrix* (1999), with the runways filled with hi-shine liquid fabrics, body-conscious catsuits and cyberpunk styling. The Artist was a passionate cinephile, with many of his favourite films such as *Blade Runner* (1982) and *Barbarella* (1968) influencing lighting, costume design and makeup during various stages of his career. It would appear *The Matrix* made a lasting impression on Prince, with the musician referencing the film often during interviews in the 2000s. Whilst presenting at Yahoo! Online Music Awards in 1999 he warned:

'…don't be fooled by the internet. It's cool to get on the computer, but don't let the computer get on you. It's cool to use the computer, don't let the computer use you. Y'all saw *The Matrix*. There's a war going on. The battlefield's in the mind. And the prize is the soul. So just be careful. Be very careful.'[4]

Prince gave an interview to *Paper* magazine in June 1999 and referred to *The Matrix* once more, likening the film to the music industry.

'The record business is like *The Matrix*. All the levels keep dissolving until you can't see what's behind anything. I'm not against the record industry. Their system is perfect. It benefits the people who it was designed to benefit: the owners.'[5]

These admissions signified the ongoing struggles of Prince and the commerciality of the music industry. Even as an early advocate of the internet The Artist had a complicated relationship with the medium due to copyright issues and artistic control.

The film also undoubtedly found its way into Prince's wardrobe. Cover art for *Rave Un2 The Year 2000* concert film could be viewed as the musician's homage to the film's female lead Trinity (Carrie-Anne Moss), albeit with a white faux fur coat in place of the black PVC trench coat (Prince had already done that in 1987). To finish the look, he wore blue-tinted wrap-around sunglasses, not dissimilar to the iconic eyewear worn in *The Matrix*. Costume designer Kym Barrett discussed the liquid-like visuals of Trinity's skintight cat-suit as mimicking the character's quick-paced combative existence, 'something like mercury, that you can't catch, it moves so quickly through your fingers'.[6] Prince's two-piece ensemble was produced in moiré like stretch fabric, a pattern with a multi-dimensional wavy watered appearance embossed into the cloth using steam. Although his performative needs differed from Neo (Keanu Reeves) and Trinity, the second-skin costume came alive under camera lights, appearing in motion with every moment and commanded a strong stage presence – perfect for a performer.

Visually, the lurid futuristic electric blue fabrics of *Rave* echo the vivid lamé purple trench coat worn in the '1999' music video and subsequent tour. At the time, Prince was photographed wearing a small number of referential outfits harking back to *1999* and *Purple Rain* including an extended lace tunic with ruffled placket and cuffs worn with a multi-tone sequin duster coat designed by Arellanes. The designer acknowledged the career-retrospective influences within these new designs, explaining he wanted to inject his signature stretch, slinky fabrics into Prince's iconic ruffles to allow a unique take on the design. Prince loved these designs and asked Arellanes for them in different colours including red, blue, white and silver.[7] By this point, Prince was experimenting with contemporary youth fashion trends, career-throwbacks and Eastern dress, the Arellanes designs allowing him to reference his previous iconic looks but in a innovative, fashion-forward way for the new millennium.

Moving into the year 2000, Prince announced that he would no longer be known as O(+> and would revert back to his own name. As he became further involved in the Jehovah's Witness religion, his style also became a bricolage of Eastern inspired kaftans, fuzzy turtle-necks and New Age ear cuffs. It seemed like there was change on all fronts. The new millennium saw a taming of Prince, more restrained and conventional; the Y2K bug had soon left his system, taking his glittery hairspray with it – for a time, at least.

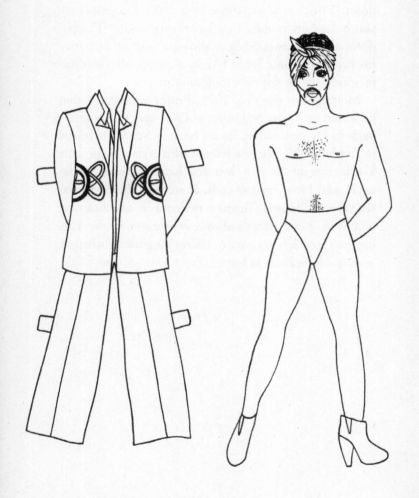

Chapter 9:
Super Bowl

On 4 February 2007, Prince went head-to-head with Mother Nature, in a performance of a lifetime on the world's biggest stage – the Super Bowl XLI Halftime Show. What resulted was the perfect performance that honoured Prince's prolific back catalogue, musical influences and contemporaries. Millions of people tuned in to watch the show, and it is now revered as one of the all-time greatest Super Bowl performances to date. A freak storm in Miami resulted in a truly once in a lifetime show that saw Prince and his band perform live on stage as the heavens opened. How was no one electrocuted? What magic slip-proof heels did Prince have on that night? Could you tell me what waterproof mascara was he wearing?

Up to this point, Prince had enjoyed varying degrees of success in the early 2000s, with his twenty-eighth studio release *Musicology* topping the charts in 2004. The project was a homage to Prince's musical heroes like Sly Stone, James Brown and Earth, Wind and Fire, to name a few. Stylistically, the album was a visible throwback into the bygone era with Prince reclaiming his place within funk royalty, dressing to the nines with coordinating cravats and cufflinks. During the same year, Prince's eye-wateringly phenomenal guitar solo amidst a performance of 'While My Guitar Gently Weeps', a tribute to the late George Harrison at Prince's Rock and Roll Hall of Fame induction ceremony, is widely regarded as one of the greatest solos of all time, with 97 million YouTube views and counting. For a Prince fan, this time was incredibly gratifying with a series of seminal live performances, and his legacy within the industry being widely acknowledged and celebrated.

Technologist and Prince scholar Anil Dash discusses the nuance within Prince's setlist on the night of the Super Bowl, particularly the additions of songs by Black artists Ike and Tina Turner, and Jimi Hendrix, noting, 'It was, in many ways, a reclamation of rock & roll as Black music, taking back a song by performing it better than the artist who wrote it.'[1] We must also acknowledge that on arguably the most important night in the musician's career, once more Prince went on stage in his durag. Weather conditions and vanity influenced Prince's decision to protect his freshly curled locks but ultimately, in wearing the durag, he chose to amplify his lived experiences as a Black man on the greatest stage of his career.

Effortlessly skimming across the water-logged stage, Prince looked otherworldly. His long-term hairstylist Kim Berry witnessed the phenomenon in person. In sheer disbelief at what she was seeing, she exclaimed, 'That man was pure magic. He was one that could dance underwater and not get wet.'[2] His skin appeared luminous with droplets of rainwater, yet his clothing seems to repel the incessant storm conditions. The only give away that Prince's outfit was within this godly realm was his floor-length trouser hems that gradually soaked up water during the performance. As the crescendo builds, Prince throws his durag off into the crowd, sweeping through his hair just once to ensure its godliness. Unable to completely shy away from previous stage antics, he strikes a phallic pose behind a fluttering white sheet. Over 100 complaints were received by the Federal Communications Commission concerning Prince's apparent suggestive guitar silhouette.[3] Prince ends the twelve-minute performance with a spine-tingling climax of 'Purple Rain' literally in a deluge of glorious purple lit rainwater.

Historically, male Super Bowl performers such as Paul McCartney, Bruno Mars, Coldplay, The Who, Bruce Springsteen and Justin Timberlake opt to wear monochromatic outfits, typically consisting of deconstructed suits and flashy streetwear in widely accepted menswear fabrics such as denim, leather and shirting. Unsurprisingly, Prince was an exemption to this trend, instead choosing to perform on stage wearing a bespoke turquoise suit, tangerine orange blouse and matching heels. Looking back the colour combination, turquoise and black pops up heavily within the *Lovesexy* era (discussed in Chapter 5) with the inclusion of orange featuring in his upcoming *3121* album release. The high-contrast appliqués worked particularly well on stage. Strategically placed at Prince's natural waist, the ornate appliqués, almost bearing resemblance to traditional Celtic knots, resulted in a defined, slight waist and torso. The design snakes its way onto the back of the suit jacket, creating graphic curves that meet at the centre back resulting in a look that works beautifully from every angle. Both the shirt and jacket collars are worn upwards, concealing his neck and framing his face. The outfit was naturally accessorised by four electric guitars, each iconic and representative of Prince's career to that point. Lit up by the ultra-violet Love Symbol stage and thousands of waving lights, Prince appears almost day-go in the storm.

Paisley Park head curator Angie Marchese cites the Super Bowl look as her favourite outfit in the archive, explaining, 'As soon as you look at it, it not only puts Prince at a place in time, but it puts you in a place at time.'[4] Similarly to fan relationships between earlier iconic outfits of the 1980s and 1990s, the Super Bowl suit signalled the arrival of a new iconic Prince for a fresh audience. Whilst the suit is modest in terms of the musician's sartorial back catalogue, the outfit is often cited as one of the more memorable looks from the Super Bowl's performers, including Lady Gaga's gravity-defying celestial bodysuits and Janet Jackson's scandalised wardrobe malfunction at the hands of Justin Timberlake.

Ultimately, the suit was a monumental success for Prince. A seemingly conservative outfit that was capable of extraordinary things. Colour-clashing turquoise and tangerine has proved to stand the test of time with the outfit remaining as one of Prince's most celebrated looks. Social anthropologist Joshua M. Bluteau states 'suits are highly semiotic garments, and while of course they are relational to the wearer, this symbiotic composite of wearer and cloth, person and crafted social self, allows for a whole tapestry of social relationships to be mitigated, and inferences of power to be woven.'[5] Much like the cloud suit, the Super Bowl ensemble is forever affiliated with Prince's flawless showmanship displayed at the legendary sporting event. Now suspended in time, stored within the walls of Paisley Park, the suit remains a sartorial marker within the musician's legacy. Following the performance, Ruth Arzate, Prince's manager at the time, remembered their conversation, proclaiming to Prince that he had just made history. He replied, 'I always make history.'[6]

Chapter 10:
Third Eye

On the cover of *Art Offical Age*, from underneath Afro-futuristic three-lens sunglasses, Prince stares out into his audience. In September 2014, Prince simultaneously released *Art Official Age* alongside *Plectrumelectrum* with his all-female rock band 3RDEYEGIRL (Ida Nielsen (bass/vocals), Hannah Welton (drummer/vocals) and Donna Grantis (guitar/vocals)). Around 2012, Prince began to grow out his natural hair and adopt a striking rock'n'roll style harking back to his teen idols Jimi Hendrix and Santana. Experimental styling began to trickle into his wardrobe once again, following a largely conservative few years of unconventional Prince tailoring. He wore brightly coloured digitally printed tunics, often bearing his likeness, as well as trippy depictions of lotus flowers, fire and electricity layered over solid turtlenecks – perhaps a practical decision to thwart off the cold or a personal styling quirk in keeping with his preference for neck concealment. On stage, he began to wear a futuristic gold visor alongside his now-signature ear cuffs he adopted in the 1990s, influenced by photographer Steve Parke. Prince was evolving once more, resulting in the psychedelic spiritual rock titan we know now today.

Originally, the far-out eyewear existed only digitally, within the *Art Official Age* album cover, but Prince wanted the real thing. Whilst visiting Paisley Park in 2014, Prince invited Corianna and Brianna Dotson, known as designer duo Coco and Breezy, to hang out and listen to his latest record. It was here Prince enquired if the sisters could make him a pair of sunglasses, but with an additional lens. They recalled, 'He asked us to design a sunglass that would cover his "third eye," a spiritual state of enlightened creativity which he believed he possessed. Breezy showed him her sketches, and he said they were exactly what he wanted—a round sunglass with a third round lens attached above the bridge.'[1] Debuting on Saturday Night Live on 1 November 2014, Prince performed in his '3rdEYEGLASS' eyewear with 3RDEYEGIRL literally the day they were shipped from the factory.[2] Prince looked every inch the rock god, decked out in leather, fringe and sporting an increasingly wide afro. Prince encouraged the sisters to reproduce the style for his fans and reassured them he did not expect anything in return. This collaboration with Prince is indicative of the musical's lifelong desire to support and nurture Twin Cities talent, with the pair growing up in Minneapolis. It is unusual to note that Prince actively encouraged the designers to make his bespoke sunglasses available to the public, defiantly going against the grain of the coveted exclusivity of luxury brands in favour of championing a young independent business. Historically, Prince had agreed many lucrative fashion deals, including a partnership with Madchester style innovator Joe Bloggs in the early 1990s to create a NPG street-wear collection and prestige ski-wear brand Metropolis by Couloir in 1996-7. With design amendments, Coco and Breezy reproduced the design, naming the style 'Tres' with a removable third lens for everyday wear (not everyone needs the protection of their third eye).

The third eye sunglasses represented an increasingly esoteric influence on Prince's work. The design's large circular lenses mimic the full moon and act as a talisman for the similar style two-lensed sunglasses The Kid wore thirty-year prior in *Purple Rain*. In the film, The Kid wears the bug-eyed mirrored eyewear as an intimidation tactic when he first meets the film's love interest, Apollonia (Patricia Apollonia Kotero) inside the packed floors of First Avenue. He uses the sunglasses as an extension of his character's bravado, pouting bemused as he delights in antagonising the singer with his childish taunts and nonsensical cocksure flirting. The extravagant glasses matched The Kid's arrogance perfectly – of course, Prince was the type to wear sunglasses indoors! By 2014, Prince had eclipsed the success he found back in 1984, cemented his place within popular culture and was now existing within the realm of music royalty. Thirty years later, Prince had commissioned a pair of sunglasses to protect his 'third eye'. Now Prince was looking, literally, inside and beyond himself.

From 2012, Prince worked with Call and Response, the Toronto-based design duo Lori Marcuz and Cathy Robinson, to create timeless highly embellished and textural garments firmly placed within the 1960s and 1970s counter culture. Their brand ethos is 'design without boundaries' which, unsurprisingly, worked well with Prince.[3] 'We worked independently and yet creatively together. He never dictated what we should create and left us to design. So, we did our research,' explains Marcuz.

'We plugged into his influences – from Sly and the Family Stone to Hendrix and Miles Davis. We listened to music and cut and sewed. No drawings were rendered, no moods boards, no stipulations – it was guerrilla design. Prince was an intensely private, singular and complex man. We strove to make garments that reflected that.'[4]

Call and Response's designs are extremely tactile with layers of cut leathers, embellishment and textural fringe mounted together to form a garment that appears lived in, just like a well-loved and lived-in leather jacket. As *Vogue* described, 'everything they made for him was deliberately aged, elegantly threadbare and baroque'.[5] Similarly to Arellanes, Prince's assistant would call the store and request designs, with Call and Response never meeting their client once. They would study YouTube clips to assess the fit of the garments, tweaking the next batch to fit his body just right. The Call and Response designs were a unique spotlight within Prince's sartorial legacy due to their artisanal, bespoke artistry. So much detail was poured into each surface area, 'they scissored Rajasthani wall hangings into patchwork jackets, or overlaid metallic leather with fringe and cording, or washed and overdyed brocade until it felt like lace.'[6] Call and Response tapped into the musician's creative energy. When discussing the complexities of the highly skilled textile embellishment, they note, 'The overlay work just evolves. It's hard to describe, but we put on music, and literally go into a fugue. I wanted to control textiles the way he controlled music.'[7] These garments were not pristine in the sense of his former Paisley Park tailored suits or stretch jumpsuits. Call and Response's elevated designs could be likened to the rough and ready experimental clothing worn by Prince on his rise to fame in the late 1970s and early 1980s – both looks expressing an element of raw creativity that was distinctive in Prince's often polished appearance. Working with Prince had a lasting impact on the designers, when discussing the whirlwind creative process, Marcuz recalled a relentless workload but looked back positively on the experience. 'What we did do was experience flow – he unleashed in us a level of creativity and freedom we had never been experienced.'[8] Many of Prince's most important moments in his later life were spent wearing Call and Response including the front cover of *V* magazine in 2013 and the 2015 Grammys, where he famously proclaimed, 'Like books and Black lives, albums still matter'.[9]

Piano & A Microphone, Prince's final tour, opened on 16 February 2016 in Melbourne and ended shortly after, on 14 April in the Fox Theatre, Atlanta. Setlists for these shows included rarely performed songs from Prince's chronological back catalogue and featured unusually intimate personal anecdotes from his past. The tour wardrobe consisted of coordinating slash neck bell-sleeved tunics and flared trousers, with printed designs. Prince wore these garments more or less solely throughout the tour with the addition of gold jewellery, a gilet, asymmetrical leather jacket and branded beanie hat. The key look from the tour was a purple two-piece with the lunar phases printed on the chest and sleeves. Garments were draped to Prince's bespoke measurements with a noticeably increased relaxed feel in the absence of visible fastenings, darts and padding. No longer performing in heels, Prince, naturally, wore stacked white platform light-up wedge trainers. It could be possible that Prince opted to wear looser fitting, less-tailored garments exclusively during the tour due to chronic pain from ongoing hip issues throughout his life. Graphic illustrative details such as the waxing and the waning of the moon printed upon his sleeve could be easily read whilst performing sat at his piano. The performances were described as intimate – a word not often used to describe a Prince show – but the musician's reflective familiarity and openness proved the tour to be ultimately a wholly unique experience with one of the world's most renowned performers. Kinetic geometric shapes warped and weaved around the colossal black graphic Love Symbol stage backdrop, evoking the hypnotic psychedelia of the '60s. Prince became part of the esoteric iconography. A Technicolour kaleidoscope, in perpetual motion that enveloped the musician as he performed on his custom purple Yamaha piano. This melding between star and stage visually signified the musician's inter-connectivity with legacy, performance and audience. This tour was history in the making.

Symbolism was ever-present in Prince's catalogue of work featuring throughout the years with ankhs, evil eyes, mandalas, and the Eye of Horus. Towards the end of his life, Prince appeared to be fascinated with lunar phases, an intriguing contradiction, considering the musician believed time to be a construct. The waxing and the waning of the moon relate to cycles of nature and is traditionally linked to feminine energy. Tour merchandise features Prince's afro profile sitting in front of a full moon. Was Prince aware of his mortality at this time? Was his spirituality taking him away from his Jehovah Witness beliefs? At this time, it was reported that Paisley Park now had a 'Galaxy Room' designed for meditation and 'illuminated entirely by ultraviolet lights and [...] paintings of planets on the walls'.[10] The third eye allows a consciousness beyond ordinary awareness. Speaking to *The Guardian* in November 2015 he discussed the 'out-of-body experience' he felt whilst playing, explaining he felt at one point as if he was sitting in the audience watching himself on stage. He continues, "That's what you want. Transcendence. When that happens,' – he shakes his head – 'Oh boy."[11] Prince had previously discussed this experience in 2014, saying, 'You reach a plane of creativity and inspiration. A plane where every song that has ever existed and every song that will exist in the future is right there in front of you.'[12]

Ongoing spiritual journeys appeared to result in a coming of home for Prince. His appearance seemed to hark back to his teenage years in North Minneapolis.

Looking at the star, you would not be amiss to see striking similarities to the iconic images of the young Prince dressed in bell-bottoms and globular afro by Robert Whitman in the late 1970s. He was dressing in the style of the musicians he admired growing up – a distinctly nostalgic style that Prince often claimed disinterest in. Prince had returned home – spiritually and visually. The clothes here are crucial to Prince's real-time legacy-making, reflective of his North Minneapolis upbringing and his ever-expanding journey of spirituality. As he explained to *The Daily Telegraph, Australia*, 'This show is 4 me, the fans and history'.[13]

Prince transitioned under the pink cherry moon on 21 April 2016.

Conclusion

The fashion world joined the wider world in mourning after Prince's sudden passing. Following his death, friend and collaborator Donatella Versace expressed to *Vogue* the impact left by him within the industry: 'He showed to men what playing with your own image really meant. He showed men how to dare and, most importantly, to not be afraid to be who they are. He ignored rules, he did what made him feel good without caring of people's judgement.'[1] Prince was not bound to societal expectations – he wore what he liked, and he looked damn good. As a result, Prince will always be revered as a style vanguard, no one did it like His Royal Badness.

Prince's legacy is limitless. In studying Prince's clothing, we begin to understand more about him as a performer, artist and as a man. His ancestry, childhood, ambitions, beliefs are all reflected within his dress. Prince used fashion not only for self-expression but as a tangible visual language. Sometimes he shocked and scandalised. Other times he appeared to use clothing as a branded signifier of his art, announcing album releases and promoting projects through both hidden and visible messages. Personal style came naturally to Prince, just like his infinite musical prowess. At the height of productivity, the Paisley Park wardrobe department operated harmoniously in sync with Prince's prolific output – churning out expressive, innovative and experimental fashion for not just himself but his protegees, friends, family and his fans. He delighted in the art of dressing and was extremely appreciative of the purple army of designers, seamstresses, pattern cutters, stylists, dyers, embroiderers, graphic artists, hair stylists and make-up artists that all worked collaboratively to bring his unique sartorial point of view to life.

For many, Prince's sartorial legacy has been a catalyst into unlocking their own artistic expression. Unsurprisingly, there is a burgeoning online community overflowing with creatives from all over the world who express their devotion to The Purple One through various artistic outlets.

Originally a paper scrapbooker, Bonnie Freshour channelled her grief following Prince's passing into creating tribute layouts and scrapbooks. Following an inspiring trip to Minneapolis, Freshour recreated her first Prince homage – the one-shoulder black leather motorcycle jacket worn in *Graffiti Bridge* (1990) and has continued to dye, embellish, stitch and source her very own Prince-inspired wardrobe, enjoying wearing many of her purple creations to work. Freshour started the 'Princespiration Cosplay' Facebook group and the worldwide community now share their creations and source materials together.[2] Fashion designer, co-host of interactive web-series *The Purple Paradigm*, and life-long fan Robin Shumays grew up listening to Prince records, thanks to her older brother who worked in the music industry and sent his sister the latest purple releases in the 1980s. Whilst Shumays has never recreated any of his looks, she does find his influence popping up in unexpected ways – from the cut of a halter neck gown to a luxe lining detail, Prince remains a constant within her creative practice.[3] Troy Gua is the mastermind behind Le Petit Prince, a project of 'lovingly detailed and meticulously staged photographs – a surreal reimagining, in sculptural miniature, of the life and career of Prince Rogers Nelson.'[4] Gua even learned how to pattern cut and sew together the tiny outfits to astounding levels of accuracy. He explains how Prince's style has impacted him, explaining, 'On a personal note, paired with a strong streak of vanity and impeccable self-grooming handed down from my Dad, Prince's fashion and sartorial legacy has always given me the confidence to be bold in my own sartorial self-expression.'[5]

Prince's music has remained an unwavering presence in my life. As a teenager I stared endlessly at his peculiar visage on the charity shop tapes, studying each era's distinct dress, font, colour palette – I was fascinated by the weird and wonderful Paisley Park universe he sang from. As a student, Prince got my friends and I on the dancefloor, perfecting our poorly coordinated 'Circle of Prince' dance routine we gleefully displayed anytime we got the Union to play 'Kiss'. It proved tricky at first but after many drunken requests, the DJs of the Scottish Borders took the hint and came prepared with Prince's back catalogue. When he eventually summoned me to Minneapolis, the city he was so fiercely proud of, I felt an immediate kinship with all the purple fans who had poured into the doors of Paisley Park from all corners of the globe. Prince has a unique way of bringing people together and it's usually the best kind of people – the weirdos, the creatives, the other. I am forever grateful to be part of that community.

For many, fashion can be viewed as a frivolity. Not Prince. He understood the importance dress can have on the everyday, not just as an internationally renowned musician. Clothing is so intrinsic to who we are. As I studied his wardrobe, a greater level of understanding of the musician was revealed. Personal quirks, influential relationships, body image. For someone like Prince, I believe fashion was a vehicle that allowed him to do what he did – it was every part as intrinsic to his creative process as a recording session or dance rehearsal.

To me, Prince represents the potential of limitless self-expression when one is wholly and uniquely themselves. His unbridled conviction to glamour has been massively influential to me growing up, particularly at a time when I was discovering my own personal style. Every look tells a story – every inch meticulously preened and polished. Unlike many other stars, Prince was seldom seen dressed in anything less than sartorial perfection. There were no creased jogging bottoms, no unkempt stubble or bedhead. A 24/7 effortless elegance akin to Bacall I can only dream to possess. Especially after the soft-jersey comforts of the COVID-19 pandemic. The patron saint for the chronically overdressed and unbothered. He did not suffer fools gladly, especially if they had the audacity to wear jeans. His feracious work ethic remains a constant reminder for me to keep forging ahead and attempt to present myself the way I feel inside. Whilst I may not look as good as Prince does in a tailored assless yellow suit I can sure as hell try. It is what he would have wanted.

Through fashion, Prince built his sonic empire, tore down societal expectations, created his own dystopian worlds, broke the expected banality of menswear, all whilst remaining in control of his own narrative. He designed his own artistic life. Prince said so himself: he was a man of exquisite taste, someone who appreciated the intricacies of fashion and always respected those who lived in their authenticities. Today, His Royal Badness' presence within fashion is still very much seen in the boundless style expression of performers such as Janelle Monae, Lil Nas X, Andre 3000, Lizzo and Harry Styles, to name a few following the same sartorial path blazed by Prince. As younger generations begin to immerse themselves into the world of The Purple One, I firmly believe his sartorial legacy will grow to gain the same depth of appreciation as his music. It is no less than Prince, and the expansive team behind making these creations a reality, deserves.

An artist in all senses of the word, I can only hope that this Greatest Hits tour of one of the greatest wardrobes to have graced the global stage sparks your own interest, and results in injecting a bit of purple splendour into your own style repertoire.

References

Introduction

1. 'Prince's False-Eyelashes Flasher in Fuchsia Lamé (as in la-me) may be the most wonderful new physical image in American pop since Bob Dylan's Electric-haired Troubadour in Winklepickers period of the mid-'60s.' Mehdelsohn, John. 'Eleganza: The Best-Dressed List'. *Creem*, Sept. 1983, www.rocksbackpages.com/Library/Publication/creem.

Chapter 1: Leg Warmers

1. "From the Archives: 18-year-old Prince signs first record deal." Bob Protzman, *Twin Cities Pioneer Press*, 21 April. 2016, www.twincities.com/2016/04/21/prince-signs-first-record-deal/. Accessed 9 June 2021.
2. Chazz Smith. Personal interview. 21 March 2018.
3. *Becoming Prince*. becoming.prince.com/map/capri-theater/. Accessed 9 June 2021.
4. Steele, Valerie. (1997). "Anti-Fashion: The 1970s." *Fashion Theory*, Vol. 1, No. 3, pp. 279–295. doi. org/10.2752/136270497779640134
5. Ronin, Ro. *Prince: Inside the Music and the Masks*. London: Aurum Press Ltd, 2012, pp. 9.
6. Thorne, Matt. *Prince*. London: Faber and Faber, 2012, pp. 23.
7. "Minneapolis – Lowest Temperature for Each Year." *Current Results*, www.currentresults.com/Yearly-Weather/USA/MN/Minneapolis/extreme-annual-minneapolis-low-temperature.php. Accessed 9 June 2021.

8.   "Put on layers of clothes, lower the thermostat and save a bundle." *The Minneapolis Star,* 25 January 1979.

9.   *RR Auction.* www.rrauction.com/search/results/?nav-search=true&str=susannah+melvoin&cp=past-auctions. Accessed 9 June 2021.

10.   "Interview: Andre Cymone "We never lost a battle of the bands"." *Funk-U,* 21 April 2017, www.funku.fr/en/2017/interview-andre-cymone-we-never-lost-a-battle-of-the-bands/. Accessed 9 June 2021.

11.   Ibid.

Chapter 2: Trench Coat

1.   "Domestic Box Office For 1984." Box Office Mojo by *IMBD Pro,* www.boxofficemojo.com/year/1984/Top of Form

2.   "Prince Talks: The Silence is Broken." Neal Karen, *Rolling Stone,* 12 September 1985.

3.   Tudahl, Duane. *Prince and the Purple Rain Era Studio Sessions: 1983 and 1984.* Maryland: Rowman & Littlefield, 2015, pp. 321.

4.   Marie France. Personal interview. 25 April 2019.

5.   Lasanta, Eloy. "Purple Coats and Bondage Fantasy." *Prince: Before The Rain,* Minnesota Historical Society Press, 2018, pp. 182.

6.   *Star Tribune,* 29 December 1984.

7.   Taupin, Bernie. "Icons and Idols: Rock "N" Roll and Milton Verret", Lot 684, Prince Purple Rain Motorcycle Jacket, Julien's Auctions, www.julienslive.com/m/lot-details/index/catalog/279/lot/108414. Accessed 9 June 2021.

8.   Till, Rupert. (2010) "Pop stars and idolatry: an investigation of the worship of popular music icons, and the music and cult of Prince." *Journal of Beliefs & Values,* Vol 31, No. 1, pp. 72.

9.   *The New Yorker,* David Denby 13 August 1984, pp. 50.

10.   Ibid.

Chapter 3: Cloud Suit

1. "Doug Henders." *Kabinett Gallery,* www.kabinettgallery.com/doug-henders. Accessed 9 June 2021.
2. "Camouflage and Prince's 16 point list: the mad story behind the cover for Around the World in a Day." Neil McCormick, *The Telegraph,* 11 June 2020. www.telegraph.co.uk/music/artists/camouflage-princes-16-point-list-mad-story-behind-cover-around/. Accessed 9 June 2021.
3. Ibid.
4. "Uptown." Zachary Hoskins, *Prince Songs,* 9 August 2007, princesongs.org/2017/08/09/uptown/. Accessed 9 June 2021.
5. "Marylou Badeaux: Prince Around The World In A Day Album Listening Session with Warner Bros." *YouTube,* uploaded by Prince Podcast, 19 November 2017, www.youtube.com/watch?v=z1oQpXXZAVc. Accessed 9 June 2021.

Chapter 4: Heels

1. *Under the Cherry Moon,* 1986.
2. Thorne, Matt. *Prince.* London: Faber & Faber, 2008, pp.130.
3. Duff, De Angela. "Under the Cherry Moon: Prince as his most authentic self." *Prince and Popular Culture: Critical Perspectives on an Interdisciplinary Life,* eds. Dr. Kirsty Fairclough and Mike Alleyne, London: Bloomsbury, pp. 15.
4. "Prince in Cinema, As Remembered by the African American Film Critics Association." *RogerEbert.com,* 29 April 2019, www.rogerebert.com/chazs-blog/prince-in-cinema-remembered-by-the-african-american-film-critics-association. Accessed 9 June 2021.
5. Thorne, pp. 140.
6. Araya, Melay. "The Black Bacchic: Music Videos of the Diamonds and Pearls Era." Online presentation, #1plus1plus1is3 Virtual Symposium, 27 March 2021.

7. Marie France. Personal interview. 25 April 2019.

8. Messerschmidt, J. *Hegemonic Masculinity: Formulation, Reformulation, and Amplification*, London: Rowman & Littlefield, 2018.

9. "J. Hoberman on Why You Should Give Prince's 'Under the Cherry Moon' Another Chance". Tatiana Craine, *The Village Voice*, 25 April 2016, www.villagevoice.com/2016/04/25/j-hoberman-on-why-you-should-give-princes-under-the-cherry-moon-another-chance. Accessed 9 June 2021.

10. "The Self-Created Immortality of Mae West." Farran Smith Nehme, *The Criterion Collection*, 4 December 2020, www.criterion.com/current/posts/7212-the-self-created-immortality-of-mae-west. Accessed 9 June 2021.

11. Chazz Smith. Personal interview. 21 March 2018.

12. "Miles Davis, 1970." The Condé Nast Collection, *Morrison Hotel Gallery*, www.morrisonhotelgallery.com/photographs/8kfeg3/Miles-Davis-1970. Accessed 9 June 2021.

13. "Paisley Park LIVE: Behind the Scenes of the Archives." *YouTube*, uploaded by Paisley Park, 5 May 2020. www.youtube.com/watch?v=t7mL5N3G7gk&t=83s. Accessed 9 June 2021.

14. "EXCLUSIVE: Sheila E. on Prince: 'He Was in Pain All the Time, but He Was a Performer'." Antoinette Bueno, *ET Online*, 22 April 2016, www.etonline.com/news/187302_exclusive_sheila_e_says_prince_was_always_pain. Accessed 9 June 2021.

15. "Prince's Heels Elevated Him as a Style Icon." Vanessa Friedman, *The New York Times*, 22 April 2016, www.nytimes.com/2016/04/23/fashion/prince-fashion-high-heels.html. Accessed 9 June.

16. "Prince Talks: The Silence Is Broken." Neal Karen, *Rolling Stones*, 12 September 1985, www.rollingstone.com/music/music-news/prince-talks-the-silence-is-broken-58812/. Accessed 9 June 2021.

Chapter 5: Polka Dots

1. "See Prince's Legendary Outfits From His Fashion Archives: The Greatest Rock 'n' Roll Closet of All Time." Sally Singer, *Vogue*, 21 April 2018, www.vogue.com/article/inside-prince-closet-at-paisley-park-fashion-archive. Accessed 9 June 2021.
2. "Jean-Baptiste Mondino on Prince: "I was completely under his spell"." Matthew Whitehouse, *iD*, 28 September 2016, i-d.vice.com/en_us/article/3kqg9k/jean-baptiste-mondino-on-prince-i-was-completely-under-his-spell. Accessed 9 June 2021.
3. "Backstage with sex and God and Mozart." Ben Brantley, *Vanity Fair*, November 1988, archive.vanityfair.com/article/1988/11/lovesexy-prince. Accessed 9 June 2021.

Chapter 6: Butt-Out

1. "Fresh Cream." George Kalogerakis and Andréé Leon Talley, *Vogue US*, January 1992.
2. "Stacia Lang: Designing outfits for Prince and the NPG." *Podcast Juice*, The Prince Podcast, 21 November 2017, podcastjuice.net/stacia-lang-designing-outfits-for-prince-and-the-npg/. Accessed 9 June 2021.
3. Harvey, John. (2007). "Showing and Hiding: Equivocation in the Relations of Body and Dress." *Fashion Theory*, Vol. 11, No. 1, pp. 76. doi.org/10.2752/136270407779934533
4. Hollander, Anne. *Sex & Suits: The Evolution of Modern Dress*, London: Bloomsbury, 2016, pp. 67.
5. "Who Criminalized the Durag?" Brian Josephs, *GQ*, 2 March 2017, www.gq.com/story/who-criminalized-the-durag. Accessed 9 June 2021.
6. "Cream Tease." Simon Mills, *Sky Magazine*, October 1991, sites.google.com/site/prninterviews/home/sky-magazine-october-1991. Accessed 9 June 2021.
7. Ritchie, Casci. (2020). "Fashioning Prince: Bikini briefs,

trench coats and zoot suits, 1978-1991", *Critical Studies in Men's Fashion,* Vol. 7, No. 1-2, pp. 91-108. DOI: 10.1386/csmf_00019_1

8. Ritchie, Casci. (2020). "Prince the provocateur: The disruption of masculinities through the style of Prince Rogers Nelson", *Queer Studies in Media and Popular Culture*, Vol. 5. No. 2-3, pp. 221-237. DOI: 10.1386/qsmpc_00037_1

Chapter 7: Chain Hat

1. This was discovered via a conversation on Twitter with Edgar Kruize: twitter.com/EdgarKruize.

2. "Newpower Soul." *Prince Vault,* www.princevault.com/index.php?title=Album:_Newpower_Soul. Accessed 9 June 2021.

3. "Prince Promotes Peace at Baltimore Show: "The System is Broken"." Evan Serpick, *Rolling Stones, 11* May 2015, www.rollingstone.com/music/music-live-reviews/prince-promotes-peace-at-baltimore-show-the-system-is-broken-188895/. Accessed 9 June 2021.

4. "Stacia Lang: Designing outfits for Prince and the NPG." *Podcast Juice,* The Prince Podcast, 21 November 2017, podcastjuice.net/stacia-lang-designing-outfits-for-prince-and-the-npg/. Accessed 9 June 2021.

5. Ibid.

6. Glynn, Prudence. *Skin to Skin: Eroticism in Dress*, Oxford: Oxford University Press, 1982, pp. 79.

7. "A King's Ransom for Prince: Artist Signs Record $100-Million Contract with Warner." Chuck Philips, *Los Angeles Times*, 4 September 1992, www.latimes.com/archives/la-xpm-1992-09-04-fi-6479-story.html. Accessed 9 June 2021.

8. "Message from The Artist." Anil Dash, *Medium,* 16 May 2016, medium.com/@anildash/message-from-the-artist-c611535da21c#.fh3jz8mi5. Accessed 9 June 2021.

9.   "Prince: Conscious and Strategic Representations of Race."
      Twilia, L. Perry, *Prince and Popular Music: Critical Perspectives on
      an Interdisciplinary Life*, London: Bloomsbury, 2020, pp. 190.

Chapter 8: Rave

1.   Parke, Steve. *Picturing Prince*, Cassell, 2017, pp. 90.
2.   Jose Arellanes. Personal interview. 3 April 2021.
3.   Ibid.
4.   "Don't be fooled by the internet: this week in tech, 20 years
      ago." Adi Robertson, *The Verge*, 20 July 2019, www.theverge.
      com/2019/7/20/20699197/this-week-in-tech-20-years-ago-
      prince-blair-witch-emachines. Accessed 9 June 2021.
5.   "The Artist Speaks Out On…Prince, Sex, Music, God and the
      Millennium." Beth Coleman, *Paper*, June 1999, sites.google.
      com/site/themusicinterviewarchive/prince/prince-1999-
      paper-magazine-interview. Accessed 9 June 2021.
6.   "Allure of the Trench Coat: That "Matrix" Look." Ruth La
      Ferla, *NY Times*, 4 May 2003, www.nytimes.com/
      2003/05/04/style/allure-of-the-trench-coat-that-matrix-look.
      html. Accessed 9 June 2021.
7.   Ibid.

Chapter 9: Super Bowl

1.   "How Prince won the Super Bowl." Anil Dash, *Anil Dash*, 4
      February 2021, anildash.com/2021/02/05/how-prince-won-
      the-super-bowl/. Accessed 9 June 2021.
2.   "Pure Magic: The Oral History of Prince's Super Bowl XLI
      Halftime Show." Alan Siegel, *The Ringer*, 29 January 2020,
      www.theringer.com/music/2020/1/29/21112539/prince-half-
      time-show-oral-history-super-bowl-xli. Accessed 9 June 2021.
3.   "Prince's Miami Super Bowl show set halftime's gold standard.
      This is how it happened", David Wilson, *Miami Herald*, 31

January 2020, www.miamiherald.com/sports/nfl/super-bowl/article239562813.html. Accessed 9 June 2021.

4. "Inside Prince's Paisley Park Archives: 7,000 Artifacts Cataloged, Many More to Go." Michaelangelo Matos, *The New York Times,* 20 April 2017, www.nytimes.com/2017/04/20/arts/music/prince-paisley-park-archives.html. Accessed 9 June 2021.

5. Bluteau, Joshua M. "The Devil is in the Detail: Why Men Still Wear Suits." *Dandy Style: 250 Years of British Men's Fashion,* eds. Shaun Cole and Miles Lambert, pp. 64.

6. "Pure Magic: The Oral History of Prince's Super Bowl XLI Halftime Show." Alan Siegel, *The Ringer,* 29 January 2020, www.theringer.com/music/2020/1/29/21112539/prince-halftime-show-oral-history-super-bowl-xli. Accessed 9 June 2021.

Chapter 10: Third Eye

1. "Twinning Combination", Christine Yeh, *20/20*, July 2017, www.2020mag.com/article/twinning-combination. Accessed 9 June 2021.

2. "Coco and Breezy on How Prince Changed Their Lives Forever With a Single Pair of Sunglasses." Adele Chapin, *Racked*, 27 April 2016, www.racked.com/2016/4/27/11505582/prince-coco-breezy-third-eye-sunglasses. Accessed 9 June 2021.

3. *Call and Response*, www.callandresponseclothing.com/. Accessed 9 June 2021.

4. Call and Response, Personal interview. 30 April 2021.

5. "See Prince's Legendary Outfits From His Fashion Archives: The Greatest Rock 'n' Roll Closet of All Time." Sally Singer, *Vogue*, 21 April 2018, www.vogue.com/article/inside-prince-closet-at-paisley-park-fashion-archive. Accessed 9 June 2021.

6. Jose Arellanes. Personal interview. 3 April 2021.

7. Ibid.

8. Call and Response, 2021.

9. "Prince: "Like Books and Black Lives, Albums Still Matter" | Recording Academy Remembers." *YouTube*, uploaded by Recording Academy / GRAMMYs, 21 April 2016, www.youtube.com/watch?v=K3_f3Wp9wSo. Accessed 9 June 2021.

10. "Prince: "Transcendence. That's what you want. When that happens – Oh, boy." Alex Petridis, *The Guardian*, 12 November 2015, www.theguardian.com/music/2015/nov/12/prince-interview-paisley-park-studios-minneapolis. Accessed 9 June 2021.

11. Ibid.

12. "A Rare Prince Interview From the ESSENCE Archives." Cheo Hodari Coker, *Essence* (June Edition) 5 May 2014, www.essence.com/celebrity/prince-interview-cover-story-essence-archives-june-2014/. Accessed 9 June 2021.

13. "Prince on his concert tour in Australia: 'This show is 4 me, the fans and history'." Kathy McCabe, *The Daily Telegraph Australia,* 6 February 2016, www.dailytelegraph.com.au/entertainment/music/prince-on-his-concert-tour-in-australia-this-show-is-4-me-the-fans-and-history/news-story/7cd970aec95e3b1f9181a44dadd460db. Accessed 9 June 2021.

Conclusion

1. "Donatella on Prince: "He Didn't Just Influence My Work, He Epitomized What Versace Stands For."" Nicole Phelps, *Vogue*, 19 April 2018, www.vogue.com/article/prince-donatella-versace-influence. Accessed 19 June 2021.

2. Bonnie Freshour. Personal interview. 26 March 2021.

3. Robin Shumays. Personal interview. 25 March 2021.

4. *Le Petit Prince.* troygua.com/le-petit-prince. Accessed 19 June 2021.

5. Troy Gua. Personal interview. 30 March 2021.

Acknowledgements

Firstly, I'd like to say thank you to my Mum and Dad for always encouraging my weird and wonderful obsessions and leaving all those Prince tapes lying around the house.

Writing this book has been something I've wanted for so long and I cannot thank 404 Ink enough for turning this pipe dream into a reality. Thank you Heather McDaid and Laura Jones for your expertise, knowledge and enthusiasm during this process, it's been invaluable.

Thank you Chazz Smith for so generously sharing your family's story with me at the very beginning of my research journey.

Marie France, Jose Arellanes, Cathy Robinson and Lori Marcuz of Call and Response – thank you for your artistry and opening up your world to me. To all the designers, pattern cutters, sewists, embroiderers, shoe designers, embellishers, jewellery makers and stylists who worked with Prince – thank you for your art, you made history. Thank you Bonnie Freshour, Robin Shumays and Troy Gua for sharing your practice and keeping Prince's creative legacy alive.

Purple scholarship continues to grow – thank you Dr. Kirsty Fairclough and Dr. Sarah Gilligan for taking a chance on me many cherry moons ago and welcoming me into the conversation. I am constantly learning as a Prince fan and want to express my gratitude to fellow scholars, fans and artists for keeping the conversation going.

A special thank you to goes to Sam Gallacher who has been my very own purple cheerleader for years and worked wonders on digitising my illustrations.

This book would not be possible without the patience, support and understanding of my boyfriend Larry. Thank you for always keeping me going and jumping down many, many, Prince rabbit holes with me in the wee hours of the morning.

Lastly, thank you Prince for a lifetime of joy and endless wardrobe inspiration. We miss you.

Further Reading

Other works by Casci Ritchie about Prince's fashion:

- *Before the Rain, 1980-1984: How Prince Got 'The Look', Prince and Popular Music: Critical Perspectives on an Interdisciplinary Life*, Bloomsbury Academic, June 2020 (contributed a chapter)
- "Fashioning Prince: Bikini briefs, trench coats and zoot suits", 1978-1991, *Critical Studies in Men's Fashion* (7.1), Intellect, January 2021
- "Prince the provocateur: The disruption of masculinities through the style of Prince Rogers Nelson", *Queer Studies in Media and Popular Culture*, Intellect, February 2021
- "Christopher Tracy's Fashion Parade: A Film by Prince", *Screen Queens*, screen-queens.com/2019/06/07/christopher-tracys-fashion-parade-a-film-by-prince/
- "'Mr. Nelson: On the North Side' Passes the Microphone to Prince's North Minneapolis community", *Screen Queens*, screen-queens.com/2021/05/10/review-mr-nelson-on-the-north-side/

- "The Beautiful One: Fashioning The Kid in Purple Rain," *Housequake*, www.housequake.com/2019/07/26/the-beautiful-one-fashioning-the-kid-in-purple-rain/
- "The Purple Trench Coat and Prince's Style Revolution", *Dismantle Magazine*, dismantlemag.com/2018/09/10/purple-trench-coat-prince-style/
- "Before The Rain 1980 to 1984: How Prince Got 'The Look'", Costume Society, costumesociety.org.uk/blog/post/before-the-rain-1980-to-1984-how-prince-got-the-look

You can find more blogs about Prince on Casci's website: casciritchie.com

Print your own Prince

To download free printable versions of Casci's dress-up Prince dolls, visit

404ink.com/prince-dressup

Please do take photos and tag @404Ink when you post them on social media, we'd love to see and share them!

About the Author

Casci Ritchie is a fashion historian, writer, film pro-
grammer and doting Pomeranian mother. Her research
specializes in twentieth-century fashion from creation to
consumption with a particular interest in fashion in film,
subcultures and Prince. She is currently researching all
aspects of Prince's sartorial legacy and has presented at
conferences across the UK, Roubaix and Prince's home
city, Minneapolis. She is a staff writer for Screen Queens
and hosts Backseat Bingo, a film club in Glasgow screen-
ing cult cinema with killer style.

@CasciTRitchie | casciritchie.com

About the Inklings series

This book is part of 404 Ink's Inkling series which presents big ideas in pocket-sized books.

They are all available at 404ink.com/shop.

If you enjoyed this book, you may also enjoy these titles in the series:

The End: Surviving the World Through Fictional Disasters – Katie Goh

The End studies apocalypse fiction and its role in how we manage, manifest and imagine social, economic and political disaster and crises. What do apocalypse narratives tell us about how we imagine our place in history? Why do we fantasise about the end of the world? What does this all unveil about our contemporary anxieties?

Flip The Script: How Women Came to Rule Hip Hop – Arusa Qureshi

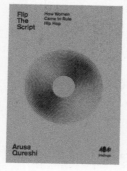

Flip The Script showcases some of the best rappers currently making music in the UK. It has taken ages for women to get the recognition they deserve in the genre, despite its beginnings in the Bronx in the 1970s – why did we take so long in the UK? *Flip The Script* gets to know the women who have paved the way, the successes and experiences of those that shape the thriving scene we have today.

Love That Journey For Me: The Queer Revolution of *Schitt's Creek* – Emily Garside

Love That Journey For Me dives deep into the cultural sensation of Canadian comedy-drama *Schitt's Creek*. Considering the fusion of existing sitcom traditions, references and tropes, this Inkling analyses the nuance of the show and its surrounding cultural and societal impact as a queer revolution.